BRITISH POLITICAL BIOGRAPHY

PETER D. G. THOMAS

LORD NORTH

ST. MARTIN'S PRESS   NEW YORK

British Political Biography
Edited by Chris Cook

Copyright © Peter D. G. Thomas, 1976

For information, write:
St. Martin's Press, Inc., 175 Fifth Avenue,
New York, N.Y. 10010

Printed in Great Britain

Library of Congress Catalog Card Number: 75-29819

First published in the United States of America in 1976

The title page drawing is reproduced
with the kind permission of the Mary Evans Picture Library

CONTENTS

PREFACE

This short political biography concentrates on the major themes of North's career: his role in Parliament, his work at the Exchequer, his performance as Prime Minister, a title which he forbade his family to use; and his policies towards Ireland, India and, above all, the American colonies. My indebtedness to previous biographies and to the many specialist studies on the period will be obvious to any reader acquainted with them. I am grateful to the authors of the unpublished theses listed in the bibliography for implicit or explicit permission to consult them; and especially to Michael Hamer for the loan of his personal copy. I owe thanks to colleagues and students at Aberystwyth: Martin Fitzpatrick read through the text and saved me from a number of errors; some new light was thrown on Lord North in undergraduate dissertations written by Margaret Jones and Timothy Brain; and Margaret White produced the typescript with such expedition that I was able to meet the publisher's deadline. Finally I am indebted to Mr F. Fortescue Brickdale and the Trustees of the Late Matthew Fortescue Brickdale for permission to use the manuscript Parliamentary Diary of Matthew Brickdale.

1

POLITICAL APPRENTICESHIP

1732–67

Frederick, Lord North, eldest son of the Earl of Guilford, was now in the thirty-eighth year of his age. Nothing could be more coarse or clumsy or ungracious than his outside. Two large prominent eyes that rolled about to no purpose (for he was utterly shortsighted), a wide mouth, thick lips, and inflated visage, gave him the air of a blind trumpeter. A deep untunable voice, which, instead of modulating, he enforced with unnecessary pomp, a total neglect of his person, and ignorance of every civil attention, disgusted all who judge by appearance, or withhold their approbation till it is courted. But within that rude casket were enclosed many useful talents. He had much wit, good-humour, strong natural sense, assurance, and promptness, both of conception and execution*

* Text has 'elocution'.

... He had knowledge, and though fond of his amusement, seemed to have all necessary activity till he reached the summit.

This was the description of Lord North by the famous contemporary commentator Horace Walpole at the moment he became Prime Minister. Walpole went on to portray North as a man who as Premier failed to fulfil the promise of his youth, blaming him for Britain's defeat in the War of American Independence: 'As a Minister he had no foresight, no consistence, no firmness, no spirit. He miscarried in all he undertook in America, was more improvident than unfortunate, less unfortunate than he deserved to be.' To Walpole and other critics of the time North was not merely the minister who lost America. He also allowed himself to be the willing tool of a King who threatened political liberty in Britain as well as America: 'He stooped to be but a nominal Prime Minister.'[1] Such comments have done much to colour historical interpretation. North had good reason to express anxiety on his deathbed about his reputation, voicing concern 'how he stood and would stand with the world. That this might be a weakness, but he could not help it.'[2] Posterity has not been kind, perpetuating his name in a stock political cliché: how many of his successors have been abused simply as 'the worst Prime Minister since Lord North'?

The popular myth has become increasingly divorced from historical opinion, with one foremost modern student of the period, John Brooke, writing of North that 'no statesman in our history has been so underrated'.[3] It is not necessary to endorse the reputed opinion of George III in 1804 that North had been the 'ablest minister and worthiest man who had ever conducted the affairs of this country'[4] to put the case for a balanced assessment. Deeper understanding of the contemporary political background has destroyed the idea that North was not a Prime Minister in his own right. Realization has come of his achievements not only at home but even overseas, where he was an eighteenth-century man confronted with nineteenth-century problems. All the difficulties of a modern empire were there: the discontent of settlement colonies, in North America; the government of the alien people of a conquered foreign colony, in Canada; rule over territories with a vast native population, in India; and the revolt of a ruling minority against its economic and political chains, in Ireland. The perspective of 200 years enables us to see that it was remarkable that North coped as well as he did with problems of this novelty and magnitude.

The North family entered upon the public stage of history in the sixteenth century, when one Edward North embarked on a successful political career that brought him a peerage as first Baron North in 1553. Later Norths fought against the Armada; chose the side of Parliament in the Civil War; and came out for Charles II at the Restoration. Thereafter the political tradition of the family was support of the Stuart monarchy, culminating in the arrest of William, sixth Baron North, for complicity in a Jacobite plot of 1722. On his release he went into exile on the Continent, dying there in 1734, when the title was inherited by the junior branch of the family from which the future Prime Minister was descended.

His great-grandfather Francis North, a younger son of the fourth Baron, rose to eminence under Charles II and ended his career by presiding over the House of Lords as Lord Keeper with the title of Baron Guilford. He also acquired by marriage the estate of Wroxton Abbey in Oxfordshire, held on permanent lease from Trinity College, Oxford. His son, second Baron Guilford from 1685 until 1729, was a prominent Tory under Queen Anne, being First Commissioner of the Board of Trade at the end of her reign. Dismissed from office and left out of the Privy Council when the accession of George I in 1714 brought the rival Whig party to permanent power, this Lord Guilford soon came to terms with political reality. In 1725 he accepted a small pension from the new dynasty, and thereafter the Norths were Whig and Hanoverian.

Our Lord North's father Francis was born in 1704. He entered the House of Commons as a Whig in 1727, and the next year married Lady Lucy Montagu, a daughter of George, Earl of Halifax, nephew and heir of the Whig Junto leader of that title. Francis North was not long in the Commons, for he succeeded his father as third Baron Guilford in 1729.* The next year he became a Gentleman of the Bedchamber to Frederick, Prince of Wales, who two years later was to be godfather to his namesake, the future Prime Minister.† Guilford owed the appointment to George II, and acted as a link between King and Prince throughout all the vicissitudes of a relationship when the son was often involved in personal and political quarrels with his father. Guilford contrived to satisfy his two masters. The Prince retained him in his household, and at the suggestion of the Princess appointed him governor to his eldest son George in 1750. When Frederick died in 1751 Guilford's services to the royal

---

* He succeeded his cousin William as seventh Baron North in 1734, and from then until 1752 was known as Lord North; but he is here referred to as Guilford.

† Contemporary scandal sometimes made the Prince North's real father, a rumour given credence by a certain resemblance between North and George III.

family were terminated by his removal from this post but rewarded the next year by the bestowal of an earldom.

North's father was to be the chief influence on his life. Guilford lived until 1790, and North consulted him until well into middle age on many important political decisions. This dependence was psychological rather than financial, although Guilford, possessed of a considerable fortune derived from inheritance and the dowries of three wives, was certainly deaf to his son's hints for assistance. Guilford was domineering as well as close-fisted. He must take both the credit for his son's upright character, and the blame for moulding a man sometimes unable to stand on his own two feet.

The Honourable Frederick North was born on 13 April 1732. His mother died when he was barely two, and in 1736 his father made a second marriage, to Elizabeth, widow of George Legge, Viscount Lewisham, who had been heir to the first Earl of Dartmouth. Frederick thereby acquired a step-brother one year older than himself in the new Lord Lewisham, who as second Earl of Dartmouth was to be his lifelong friend. The marriage was also to produce a half-brother for him in Brownlow North, and with two step-sisters and two half-sisters as well North grew up at Wroxton in a happy and devout family atmosphere. In 1742 he was sent to school at Eton, whence his father received this favourable report from the headmaster: 'I am pleased to see in many instances how both the masters and the boys love him, and that he really by his behaviour deserves it from both, which is not often the case. I think he has greatly contributed to the very good order the school is in at present.' An industrious and able pupil, North was often at the head of his form, and when he left to go to Oxford, in 1749, his father wrote: 'It gives me great pleasure to find you have left a very good name behind you, and I hope you will preserve it at Oxford.' The family connection meant that North would enter Trinity College as a matter of course, and Guilford took pains to ensure that his 'dear Fritz' would have his rooms there suitably equipped and furnished. Lewisham was already at the same college: and the presence of his pious step-brother combined with the influence of his tutor, the Reverend James Merrick, to strengthen North in his religious beliefs. On his entrance into public life he received this compliment from Merrick: 'Your improvement in piety, at this season of your life, will be the best preparation for every scene of it; and your preserving that cheerfulness of temper and desire for knowledge which you now have, may be of excellent use in recommending the example of your piety to others.'[5]

1751 was an important year for the Wroxton household. Guilford, whose second wife had died in 1746, made his third and last marriage, to the widow of the second Earl of Rockingham, a match that brought him the Waldeshare estate in Kent. Lewisham succeeded to the title and estates of his grand-father. And, as the new Lord Dartmouth, he and North left university and in July set out to complete their education by a Grand Tour, accompanied by a tutor selected for his virtue. Seldom can such a precaution have been so unnecessary! The two highly moral and dutiful young men left not a breath of scandal and created a favourable impression wherever they went. Contemporaries familiar with the clumsy Prime Minister of later life would have read with astonishment Dartmouth's report from Dresden: 'Mr North, by the ingenuity of his manners added to the comeliness of his person gained himself an universal admiration.'[6] North reported that Germany was superior for hospitality, Italy for cultural edification:[7]

The principal pleasure of a traveller in Italy is in seeing the great perfection to which the Italians have pushed the arts of painting, sculpture, and architecture. In point of view of society I think the tour of Italy inferior to that of Germany. Scarce any one of them have that easy manner of inviting foreigners to their houses and tables which they have in Germany.

Not until early in 1754, after a progress of some two and a half years through Germany, Italy and France, did the two young men arrive back in England, having acquired the polish it was the purpose of the exercise to impart. North had added urbanity and wit to his natural good humour. He could speak French, had a smattering of two or three other languages, and was well versed in history and classics. The young Lord North in 1754 was a man of integrity, high moral character, good education, excellent manners and a sense of humour. These attributes were sufficient to win universal praise from contemporaries and to offset his physical disadvantages: plumpness in face and figure, eyes that were both prominent and defective, an indistinct but loud voice, and a general clumsiness of behaviour.

The first part of North's life was over. His education complete, it was time for him to enter politics, the usual destiny for a young man of his background. His earliest surviving letter makes reference to a parliamentary by-election, and it was written at the age of eight![8] North had been born into the upper echelons of the oligarchy that governed Britain. Effective power in national and local government was in the hands of several hundred landed families, titled and untitled. They controlled the great majority of the parliamentary constituencies, both county and borough: and, according to their rank and wealth, dominated the institutions of government from the House of Lords to the county benches of magistrates. This oligarchy was broadly based and elastic, entered freely by men who had made money from commerce and industry. The norm was for a family to control or dispute no more than one or two of the 558 seats in the House of Commons. With direct government influence at elections limited to some fifty seats the House virtually comprised 500 self-returning members. Many did not greatly concern themselves with politics, having taken a seat out of family tradition or some similar motive, and were lax in their general attendance: but the House would be full at moments of political crisis. Every ministry therefore faced the problem of managing an assembly over whose composition it had little control: for although ministers owed their appointment to the sovereign, the Commons could bring about their fall by a withdrawal of confidence in such men and their measures.

Part of the answer came from the traditional method of patronage, the bestowal of honours and official salaries on M.P.s, their relatives and friends: but although most M.P.s solicited and accepted such favours to some degree, this factor never produced more than a makeweight of 100 to 150 'sure votes'. The key lay in positive leadership of the House, for modern party disciplines did not exist: a minority of M.P.s were banded together in 'factions', rough political groupings under acknowledged leaders; but the majority were proud of their 'independence', real or professed. They had to be convinced by debating performance and administrative competence that the ministers chosen by the King merited their support, and as a matter of practical politics it was highly desirable that the head of the ministry should be in the Commons, for that House did not care to be ruled from the Lords. This was a truth the new head of the ministry, the Duke of Newcastle, was just about to learn at the time North entered Parliament. The First Lord of the Treasury, his brother Henry Pelham, died while the general election of 1754 was in progress, and Newcastle decided to succeed him and govern the Commons by deputy. Newcastle was the great political manager of the age, but not all the inducements of patronage could atone for the lack of direct guidance in the Commons. The experiment was to lead to his temporary fall from office two years later as that formidable orator William Pitt savaged his ministry for mismanagement of the Seven Years' War against France.

North had returned to England in time for the general election, and he entered the Commons at the same time as Dartmouth took his seat in the Lords. There was a safe constituency ready for him, the single-member borough of Banbury, only three miles from Wroxton. Since 1734 the North family had nominated the member without opposition, and no challenge was to be made to Lord North's twelve returns for the borough. Unlike the majority of M.P.s, North entered Parliament to embark on a political career, and his claims to office were promptly and frequently pressed by his father as well as himself. It was the assumption of the British ruling class that the state should provide lush pastures upon which they could graze, and Guilford at every opportunity bombarded men of influence with requests for patronage for his son as well as a court office once again for himself. Guilford was a wealthy man and could easily have supported North out of his own pocket: but none of his contemporaries thought the worse of Guilford for his behaviour, although some of North's biographers have done.

Rarely can a young M.P. have gone to Westminster with personal connections of such potential value. His uncle, the second Earl of Halifax, was President of the Board of Trade, and Dartmouth's uncle, Henry Legge, was Chancellor of the Exchequer. North could also claim kinship with Newcastle, and had written to him on the Grand Tour as 'your cousin'. The relationship was distant: North's mother's grandfather's brother-in-law had been Newcastle's father: but it was one that both cultivated. The Duke was to help North up the vital first step of the political ladder; yet at no time did North behave as one of Newcastle's personal following. His first application for a post came when in 1756 Newcastle briefly gave way to William Pitt after the disastrous start to the Seven Years' War. During the consequent reshuffle of places North aspired to a seat at the Board of Trade under his uncle Halifax: but his solicitations proved unavailing even though Halifax and Legge used their utmost endeavours on his behalf.[9] There were too many applicants for too few places, and North had first to prove himself in Parliament before he could jump to the head of the queue. In his first years at Westminster North made no attempt to do so. Instead he got married.

As early as February 1755 it was being rumoured in London society that he had proposed to Anne Speke, daughter of a Somersetshire gentleman. No contemporary deemed her a beauty, most comments on her appearance being singularly unflattering: Lady Harcourt said that North himself was 'beautiful in comparison to the lady the world said he is to marry'.[10] Nor was she an heiress in her own right, although expected to inherit a Somerset estate worth several thousand pounds a year from an elderly relation, Sir William Pynsent. But she was a sensible and sweet-tempered girl, and was to prove an affectionate companion. They were married on 20 May 1756, when the bridegroom was twenty-four and the bride sixteen, and lived happily ever after, until North died thirty-six years later. One of their daughters subsequently recalled that she 'never saw an unkind look or heard an unkind word passed between them. His affectionate attachment to her was as unabated as her love and admiration of him.'[11]

Poverty can be relative, and the Norths soon found that their marriage settlements were not generous enough to maintain them in the style of life appropriate to their class. North's income was between £2,000 and £2,200 a year, his expenses at least £2,500: in the first three years of matrimony he contracted debts of nearly £2,000. Social aspirations were withered by the frost of economy. North wrote to his father on 1 February 1757: 'There are a great many balls this year to none of which Lady North has been invited. She endeavoured to make it up to herself by having a little accidental Hop the other night for some of her particular friends without a supper.' A year later he was contemplating abandonment of any London season and going up to town by himself for a few months of the parliamentary session. North's household bills were soon increased by the arrival of seven children, five of them in the first decade of the marriage. Grandfather Guilford sent expressions of delight, but nothing more substantial. If financial strain did not mar the domestic bliss of the North family, it provided Lord North with a spur to seek a post from government.[12] And in 1757 Newcastle helped him to enhance his prospects of office by a timely and successful parliamentary debut.

The Duke was back at the Treasury, having resolved the political crisis of 1756–7 by a coalition wherein Pitt controlled the conduct of the war and Newcastle managed Parliament; and he asked North to second the Address of Thanks in reply to the King's Speech at the beginning of the new session on 1 December 1757. Such semi-formal occasions were usually an honour and ordeal for inarticulate backbenchers rather than an opportunity for promising young men to make their mark: but North took his chance well. Guilford, home at Wroxton, soon received flattering accounts of his son's success, among them a report from veteran M.P. Charles Montagu that the maiden speech was

the subject of discourse in all companies. If anybody was sorry I fancy it was the Secretary of State [William Pitt], to have his work taken out of his hands, and to see he had so dangerous a rival. I am not singular in this notion. He possessed himself perfectly well, his language was correct and not too flowery, no hesitation from beginning to end, his action direct and proper, his voice very clear and distinctly heard everywhere, never harsh . . . a most masterly performance it was indeed.[13]

Other comments were almost as laudatory, and not only those to Lord Guilford. North himself told his father that he had spoken 'with a loud voice and a tolerable manner, and to that much more than to my matter, I owe my reputation'. It was North's presentation of his speech rather than its substance that must have struck observers as significant. His self-possession in the heat of battle was to be his greatest debating asset, and his powerful voice a valuable weapon in a House that was often noisy. Debating talent was always at a premium in the eighteenth-century House of Commons, and North's success promised immediate reward: he was at once able to report to his father an assurance from Lord Halifax that 'he looks upon me as the first claimant in case of a vacancy at the Board of Trade'.[14]

The first tender of office came not from Halifax or Newcastle, but from William Pitt. In January 1758 he offered North a post that fell within his own patronage as Secretary of State for the South – that of envoy at Turin, capital of Savoy. North was astute enough to perceive that such an appointment would be detrimental to his long-term prospects, and told his father that he had refused the offer because 'most men who have passed their youths in foreign employments make no great figure in Parliament at their return'. A man taking such a post would acquire neither parliamentary reputation nor administrative experience, and was 'likely to be more in the power of those who govern than any person who can help it would choose to be'.[15] North knew the path to power lay at Westminster, and despite his financial problems he was determined to wait for a suitable appointment. In the interval he strengthened his parliamentary claims to office, as when on 20 February 1758 he led the administration reply to an opposition motion for annual parliamentary elections.

The next year he was rewarded with an office that matched his highest aspirations. In May 1759 Newcastle informed Pitt that he proposed to nominate North to a vacancy at his Treasury Board: 'He is a near relation of mine, but I hope his appearance in Parliament will make the choice approved, and that he will be in time a very useful and able servant of the Crown.'[16] North's appointment took effect on 2 June. It must have been welcome: the salary of £1,400 meant that for the first time the income of the North family household was greater than its expenditure; and he had the guidance at the Board of two experienced patrons. Newcastle himself presided there, and Dartmouth's uncle Henry Legge was Chancellor of the Exchequer. North began to acquire the knowledge of financial matters that, allied to his parliamentary expertise, was to prove the foundation of his political success. But this promotion was also to prove a future handicap. North had leapfrogged into the Treasury over many lesser posts, including the Boards of Trade and Admiralty. He was to become Prime Minister without experience of any other government business except finance.

Out of several potential sponsors it had been Newcastle who bestowed on North his first office, and the Duke came to hope that he had acquired another promising young recruit to his personal following. Propinquity and temperament strengthened the bond during the next few years. North shared the Treasury abhorrence of Pitt's extravagant conduct of the Seven Years' War: years later he paid public tribute in the House of Commons to the Duke's conduct of national finance at this time. Newcastle had reason to regard North as one of his adherents when George III came to the throne in 1760, and frowned upon a suggestion early in 1761 that he should be promoted away from the Treasury Board. A year later, in January 1762, Newcastle confided to the Duke of Devonshire that North was 'coming to belong as much to me as anybody'.[17] He was soon to be disillusioned on this, as in so much else, when the political consequences of George III's accession unfolded themselves.

The new King's determination to appoint his favourite Lord Bute as his first minister had some immediate results. Bute replaced the nonentity Lord Holdernesse as Pitt's fellow-Secretary of State, and his personal antipathy led to Legge's dismissal as Chancellor of the Exchequer. The first crisis in the ministry came when Pitt resigned in October 1761 after failing to persuade the cabinet to declare war on Spain. Three months later that decision proved inevitable, and the Newcastle administration faced the embarrassment of explaining to Parliament the sudden change of policy. Newcastle, aware of the crucial importance of the first debate, asked North to propose the Commons Address to the King on the subject. North accepted with alacrity: 'There is no point in the world in which I have so determined an opinion as aversion to a war with Spain, but ... I think ... that you would never have engaged in the war if it could have been possible to have been avoided with honour or safety.'[18] In his speech on 19 January 1762 North portrayed the war as a regrettable necessity caused by the alliance of Spain with France, and denounced Pitt as a warmonger. Pitt made a spiritless reply, the Address was carried without a vote, and the debate enhanced North's reputation: a successful attack on a political giant was the classic path to parliamentary fame.

Four months later Newcastle himself resigned in protest against a cabinet decision to end the financial subsidy to Britain's ally Prussia, and was succeeded by Bute. North faced one of the critical decisions of his life. His own inclination was to go out with Newcastle, but he stayed on at the Treasury Board under Bute. His predicament was more complex than the selfish calculations of the many ambitious politicians and placemen who deserted Newcastle in 1762. Undoubtedly North too had to look to his own future; he was under pressure to remain in office from Lord Guilford, who was anxious not to have his own chances of court favour prejudiced; and his only close political connection was with his uncle Halifax, who remained in the ministry and soon became Secretary of State. North's decision was based on the balance of his personal loyalties, and it was one about which he remained uneasy during the year of the Bute administration.

It was not a happy time for North. There soon developed a mutual antipathy between Bute and himself: and during the last months of 1762 Bute considered various proposals of removing North from the Treasury Board by nomination to a court appointment. North remained at the Board, determined not to be diverted from an efficient office of business into what was for an ambitious politician a blind alley.[19] And in April 1763 he found matters more to his liking when Bute resigned and was succeeded by George Grenville, who became First Lord of the Treasury, Chancellor of the Exchequer, and Leader of the House. Grenville was chosen by Bute after consultation with his Commons Leader, Henry Fox, who during the negotiations made this unflattering comment on North as a man who would make himself useful to any ministry: 'Lord North is young and interested, and his views of rising in the House of Commons will, I fancy, make him I won't say tractable, but obsequious.'[20] Grenville was a man North respected and learned much from, both at the Treasury and in the Commons: and North thoroughly approved the successful fight the new ministers put up against George III's continued dependence on Bute, when in the summer of 1763 they compelled the King to put aside his favourite.[21]

The Grenville ministry saw North move significantly nearer to the centre of the parliamentary stage. During the two sessions of its existence he made some fifty recorded speeches. The most important subject was the *North Briton* affair, the first episode in the chequered career of that famous rascal and radical, John Wilkes. North's performance was to put him in the front rank of parliamentary debaters.

The *North Briton* was a weekly opposition paper run by Wilkes, then M.P. for Aylesbury. The forty-fifth number, published on 23 April 1763, attacked the King's Speech from the throne at the end of the parliamentary session in forthright language that offended George III and his ministers. Swift government action followed, instigated by North's uncle Halifax as Secretary of State. Since the publication was anonymous, Halifax, after receiving advice from the law officers of the Crown that the paper was a seditious libel, issued a general warrant on 26 April for the arrest of 'the authors, printers and publishers'. When early evidence confirmed the suspicion that Wilkes was the author he was also arrested under the general warrant, but released a few days later by Chief Justice Pratt of the Court of Common Pleas on the ground of parliamentary privilege.

The affair threatened to snowball into a major political crisis, for when Parliament met again in the autumn the House of Commons would be called upon to consider whether the arrest of Wilkes had been a breach of privilege. Newcastle's friends made clear their intention of exploiting the issue, and they would have the formidable assistance of Pitt, who was concerned about Halifax's action as an attack on both parliamentary privilege and the liberty of the press. By October Grenville had evolved a strategy to deal with the situation. His plan comprised a resolution to declare *North Briton No. 45* a seditious libel; another to declare that parliamentary privilege did not cover this offence, thereby exposing Wilkes again to legal action; and finally a motion to expel him from the Commons.

North, whose uncle was at the centre of the controversy, was asked to take the lead on the subject in the House of Commons. The request may have come directly from Halifax, for it was to him that North replied on 30 October. His letter evinced reluctance to shoulder such a responsibility for two reasons: resentment at the lack of any reward for previous services, and diffidence at undertaking such a task. 'The marks of favour received from his Majesty by my father and myself are not such as to make the world expect that we should be the first in the declaration of duty . . . I think my proper place will be to support the motion in debate than to make it.' The ministers sought to meet North's objections on both counts: adequate support was promised in debate, and Bute was blamed for the neglect of Guilford; Grenville did afterwards attempt to reward North by proposing Guilford as Lord Privy Seal, but the suggestion was vetoed by George III.[22] Within a week North had agreed to act, but he told his father that he had been driven into a position he would rather have avoided.[23]

Nothing can go more against me than the business I am now upon, but whilst things stand in their present ticklish situation it is impossible to avoid it. You may be sure that I shall be very moderate in my expressions, but that will be to no purpose. The part I take will be an unpardonable crime to the other side. I begin heartily to wish I had followed my own opinion in going out with the Duke of Newcastle.

North realized that henceforth he would be damned in the popular mind as on the side of 'tyranny' against 'liberty'. In this sense the part he played in the first Wilkes case coloured his future career in the eyes of many contemporaries and historians, Horace Walpole making this savage comment on North as 'the chief manager for the Court . . . Lord North's mouthing and boisterous manner, his coarse figure, and rude untempered style, contributed to make the cause into which he had unnecessarily thrust himself appear still more odious.'[24]

When Parliament met on 15 November North at once showed his mettle by standing up to Pitt in a dispute about the order of business. After a ministerial majority of 300 to 111 had established priority for consideration of the government case against Wilkes, North moved that the offending issue of the *North Briton* was 'a false, scandalous and seditious libel', demonstrating by detailed quotations that every part of this condemnation was justified: and the House approved the resolution after a heated debate by 273 votes to 111. On 24 November North put the motion that privilege did not cover seditious libel. He adopted the line of argument decided upon by the administration before Parliament met, that privilege did not extend to criminal matters, citing many historical precedents to prove his point. Much of his speech reflected the concern about his public image that he had mentioned to his father. He tried to show that his position put him, and not his opponents, on the side of liberty, claiming that he was arguing for equality before the law and against the establishment of a privilege that would oppress ordinary people. Parliamentary privilege, he said, was too often a licence for M.P.s and their servants to misbehave. The ensuing debate fell into the hands of the lawyers, and North took no further part in it: but the administration won by the overwhelming majority of 258 to 133.

The final part of the government programme, the expulsion of

Wilkes, was delayed by his absence through injury in a duel. Ministerial suspicions that Wilkes was malingering and did not intend to appear before the Commons seemed to be confirmed by his flight to Paris on 24 December. When the House considered the matter on 19 January 1764, North therefore moved to proceed at once in the case. The verbal and written evidence submitted to the House afforded convincing proof that Wilkes had been the author and publisher of *North Briton No. 45*: and after several debates and four divisions the expulsion of Wilkes was carried without a vote.

North had completed his allotted task in the ministerial campaign with zeal and ability: but he took little part in what proved to be the main parliamentary battle, over the legality of general warrants. Independent opinion in the Commons swung against the administration on this issue, and in February 1764 the Grenville ministry was hard pressed to avoid defeat. Yet only on 6 February did North make an important speech, reiterating the ministerial argument that if Parliament was to decide the matter the correct procedure should be through legislation and not, as proposed by the opposition, by a mere resolution of the House. He did not speak at all on the critical occasion of 17 February, when the ministry won by only fourteen votes, 232 to 218, at a division taken at six o'clock the next morning. Concern to avoid if possible undue public commitment to causes unpopular in the House of Commons was to be a characteristic of his political behaviour.[25]

If the *North Briton* case advanced North's political career, his private fortune was adversely affected by his role in the other important topic of debate that session, the controversy over a cider tax introduced in 1763. North had defended it then. He now spoke against repeal of the Cider Act on 24 January 1764, and argued strongly for keeping the tax in noisy debates of 31 January and 7 February. This behaviour cost North dear, the disinheritance of his wife by Sir William Pynsent, who as a Somerset squire shared the local resentment at the cider tax and by a late change in his will left his entire estate to William Pitt, apparently for his political services to the nation. This bequest to a man he had never met was the talk of London society after Pynsent's death on 12 January 1765: Horace Walpole heard that Pynsent had been so furious with North that he had encouraged a mob to burn him in effigy. North himself took the blow with his usual phlegm when telling his father the news: 'It is reported, and from pretty good authority that he left it all to me but altered his will in consequence of the cider tax.'[26]

North remained a leading ministerial debater in the session of

1765. The political highlight was the revival of the general warrants issue on 29 January 1765, when an opposition motion declaring the practice illegal was countered by a destructive amendment from a ministerial lawyer. North made two speeches in the debate, one of them to defend his uncle Halifax for his part in the affair. His main contribution was to put forward the stock administration argument. It was not the business of Parliament to decide a question of law, he said, and it would be wrong to do so while the matter was still before the courts.[27] The ministry won by 39 votes, and was not in danger for the rest of the session. North was later prominent in debates on the Regency Bill, and his argument on 9 May against the opposition demand for parliamentary nomination of the regent was one likely to win the approval of George III; for North urged 'the natural right of a father to choose a guardian to his child'.[28] But the most significant feature of North's speeches this session was the attention he gave to finance: and among them were his first on America, in support of the taxation of the colonies.

Although in 1769 North was to tell the Commons that he had accepted the Stamp Act 'very much' on Grenville's authority, his place at the Treasury Board must have made him thoroughly familiar with the background and details of the measure. He spoke twice in the only important debate on it, when Grenville proposed the resolutions on 6 February 1765. North reminded M.P.s of two points made earlier by Grenville, that the measure had already been postponed a year from motives of caution and of consideration for the colonies, and that there had been no colonial complaint about this particular method of taxation.[29]

North was a loyal servant of the Grenville administration in the Commons and at the Treasury until it was dismissed from office in July 1765; but unlike a number of his colleagues he had not developed any personal allegiance to Grenville. Nor had there been a bond of patronage and obligation; his father was still without the court office he so coveted, and North himself had been refused the Lord Lieutenancy of Somerset when it fell vacant in 1764.[30] When Newcastle's friends formed the new ministry under the Marquess of Rockingham they therefore hoped that North would stay in office: he was at one time thought of for Chancellor of the Exchequer, and then for the lucrative post of Joint Paymaster-General.[31] North was the only member of Grenville's Treasury Board not to be dismissed: but he resigned, this time without the heartsearching that had marked his break with Newcastle in 1762. The ministry nevertheless retained hopes of winning him over. On several occasions during the summer he told Paymaster-General Charles Townshend that he was free 'from the least degree of engagement'; Townshend subsequently repeated this to Newcastle, adding the comment that 'if obligations, though of some years standing, are unfashionably to be remembered, his will be found to lie, not on the side he quits, but on that he comes to'.[32] Townshend's opinion that 'there is no one belonging to the late administration whose talents would be of more use to the present' was shared by the cabinet. An obvious means of approach was through North's step-brother Dartmouth, who, though not usually an active politician, had agreed to become Rockingham's President of the Board of Trade: and the cabinet authorized Newcastle to ask him to approach North, the offer being the post of Joint Vice-Treasurer of Ireland, then worth £2,000 a year.[33] North refused it and began the new parliamentary session in opposition, for the first time in his career.

North's motives can only be surmised. He may have shared the widespread contemporary belief that the ministry would be short-lived; and this calculation may have been reinforced by anger at the unceremonious dismissal of the Grenville ministry, especially as his uncle Halifax had been one of the cabinet summarily ejected from office. North could not have been alienated by the American policy of the administration, for it was as yet unformulated; and there were obvious disadvantages in his decision. The loss of an official salary must have been a severe blow to a man in his financial circumstances: and Lord Guilford cannot have looked kindly on a step adversely affecting his own prospects of royal favour.

The parliamentary session of 1765–6 was dominated by the Stamp Act Crisis, the problem of the colonial resistance to Grenville's taxation that was to be resolved by the Rockingham ministry's decision to repeal the Act, ostensibly on account of the consequent economic distress in Britain. North made his own hardline position clear by two early speeches even before the administration had decided on its policy; and on 5 February 1766 he supported an opposition amendment about compensation for loyalist victims of the riots in America. He voted against the repeal on 21 February; and a significant portent of his future attitude as minister was his speech on 24 February in support of an amendment moved by lawyer Blackstone to restrict repeal to those colonies whose assemblies expunged any resolutions challenging Parliament's right of taxation. North justified this proposal as being something more than a bare assertion of Britain's authority, thus anticipating the principle of his own later argument for retention of the American tea duty.

This speech saw him use the humour that was to be one of his most effective weapons in debate: for he made an ironical comparison between Parliament's weak surrender and the spirit and dignity of the colonial assemblies.[34]

It was nevertheless a quiet session for North. He spoke once more on America, and four times on finance, opposing the ministry's repeal of the cider tax and criticizing a new window tax. But even if allowance is made for the contrast between an office-holder with obligations to defend government policy and his new role as a freelance politician in opposition, it is difficult to avoid the conclusion that North was keeping open as many options as possible. Certainly 1766 was to see political leaders seeking his support.

In May the Rockingham administration believed that the time was ripe to approach him again. North was once more offered an Irish Vice-Treasurership, hesitated whether to accept, and did so on or about 20 May. By 24 May he had changed his mind, and apologized to Rockingham 'for all my difficulties, which must have embarrassed you and my other friends, and, particularly, for this last change of opinion'. That North had realized the Rockingham ministry would not last much longer was the deduction made by Charles Jenkinson, an able man of business who had resigned from his post as Secretary to the Treasury on the dismissal of Grenville and whose future career was to be closely linked with that of North.[35] George III was indeed then waiting for Pitt's agreement to form a new administration, and when he consented to do so Rockingham was dismissed, in July 1766. Pitt took the post of Lord Privy Seal to avoid the labour of a departmental office, and chose the Duke of Grafton as his First Lord of the Treasury. He intended to take a peerage as Chatham, and had already marked out North as a valuable acquisition to his administration's debating strength in the Commons, offering him a post on 28 July:[36]

I have now the honour and pleasure to open to you by his Majesty's commands that the King would see with satisfaction Lord North return to his service. It is his Majesty's intention to make two joint Paymasters-General, and should your Lordship (fortunately for the King's service) think it agreeable to you to be one of them, I should esteem myself happier in having writ this letter . . . than in most when I have had the King's commands to employ my pen.

North told a friend that 'his office had been offered him, in such a manner, that he could have no reason to refuse it'. He may have been annoyed that he had to share it with another, and an undertone of resentment can be perceived in the jest with which he took up the appointment; walking up the steps of the Pay Office he saw the resome dog's dirt, and at once gave instructions that half this perquisite should be given to his fellow Paymaster-General, George Cooke, a favourite of Chatham. Certainly North's satisfaction had been clouded by the resignation of Dartmouth after Chatham's refusal to upgrade his post to one of Secretary of State for America, for he sent this comment to his father: 'Nothing can be more vexatious than to find myself constantly by the strange political jumbles opposed to one of the men that I honour love and esteem the most.'[37]

North's early discontent vanished as his political role became vastly more important than his office signified. He was appointed to the Privy Council on 10 December 1766, a formal acknowledgement that he was being consulted on government policy and a testimony to his role in the Commons. Here Chatham's departure for the Lords, a step North thought unwise, left as the administration spokesmen in the House the irresolute Conway, Secretary of State, and the irresponsible Charles Townshend, Chancellor of the Exchequer. The parliamentary problems of the ministry were increased by the disagreement of both men with the policy of Chatham over the chief political issue of the new session, the territories acquired by the East India Company during and after the Seven Years' War. This combination of circumstances enhanced North's importance as the prospective advocate of ministerial measures in the Commons. He was now for the first time given a formal share in deciding policy; for by early 1767 he was being called to at least some of the cabinet meetings on East India Company business, a summons certainly not warranted by his office.

The point at issue within the administration was how the government could get hold of some of the Company's revenue: all were agreed on the principle that it should do so. Chatham and his personal following favoured a parliamentary declaration that the territories belonged to the Crown, with whose military and naval aid most of them had been won: the Company would then be paid for administering them. But the collapse of Chatham's health prevented the implementation of this policy and led to a gradual disintegration of his ministry: from late in 1766 until the middle of 1769 he took little part in politics, and the burden of leadership fell on the inadequate shoulders of Grafton. Conway and Charles Townshend preferred to negotiate a settlement with the Company on the basis of proposals that would leave the Indian territories in the Company's possession in return for an annual payment to the government. By March 1767 a decision had become imperative. Chatham himself was absent from a cabinet on the subject on 3 March, but Conway and Townshend were overruled by the other six present, among them Lord North.[38]

The next day Grafton offered North Townshend's post as Chancellor of the Exchequer, Chatham having obtained the King's permission for this step. North refused, so Grafton reported to George III, because 'he saw the business too much involved for him to undertake so difficult a post'. According to a later recollection of his eldest son, who was only nine years old at the time, North paced up and down the Pay Office considering whether to accept the offer, 'it being the general opinion that the ministry could not last a month'. This political risk and the prospect of facing an angry Townshend in the Commons suffice to explain North's decision. At his suggestion every effort was made to conceal the offer, to avoid embarrassment to the ministry: but news of it leaked out, Edmund Burke assuming that Chatham's motive was to obtain a Commons spokesman for his attack on the East India Company.[39] North refused to play the part. He spoke only once in the parliamentary discussion of the subject that ended in a compromise solution. The Company agreed to pay the state the sum of £400,000 a year, and had a dividend limit of 10 per cent imposed upon it by parliamentary legislation.

North took little part in debate again that session, but when he did so it was with effect, as in a famous debate over the land tax on 27 February 1767, when an opposition amendment to reduce the tax by 1s. was carried by 206 votes to 188. North then spoke 'extremely well', according to Horace Walpole, 'and began to be talked of for Chancellor of the Exchequer', the post he was offered a week later. The administration did not challenge the resolution when it was reported on 2 March, but North engaged in a witty verbal duel with Richard Rigby, Commons spokesman for the Bedford group.[40] Later in the session North was concerned with the administration policy towards New York, which had refused to comply with the provisions of the 1765 Mutiny Act requiring each colony to supply army units based within it with various necessities. The ministerial riposte, devised by Charles Townshend, was to forbid the New York Assembly to pass any legislation until it had given way on this point.

Townshend was due to propose the appropriate resolutions to the Commons on 5 May, but he suffered an accident that day. Since Conway disapproved of the policy, Townshend sent for North and gave him his papers so that he could move the resolutions instead, an implicit recognition of North's growing stature in the Commons. Rigby opposed this step when the House met, asserting the need for the minister best informed to introduce the subject, and the matter was postponed. Horace Walpole thought that Rigby wanted to deprive North of an opportunity to shine: when Townshend moved the resolutions on 13 May North made only a short speech in support.[41] If this coercion of New York was the main point of American interest to contemporaries, it was Townshend's taxation measures that were to be of infinitely more significance in the future. North always said afterwards that he had nothing to do with the imposition of these duties on tea, paper, glass and other commodities imported into the colonies, and there is no reason to doubt his claim. He was not a member of the Treasury Board at the time, he was not summoned to the cabinet when the taxes were being considered, and he did not speak on them in the Commons.

North's debating record might appear a slender foundation for his rise to the Leadership of the House at the end of the year even if allowance is made for the paucity of parliamentary reports in the period. But appraisal of his first ten years as a speaker in the Commons provides an intelligible explanation. Surviving comments on North's speeches are almost invariably favourable; and he had been discriminating in choice of topic. He had taken care to avoid giving offence to independent opinion in the House, as by not speaking on the militia. If with reluctance North had taken a prominent role in the *North Briton* case, he had not done so on the contentious issue of general warrants. His oft-professed disdain for popularity was misleading, for he had been careful to avoid as far as possible advocacy of causes unpopular in the House of Commons.

North's Treasury experience and his prominence in financial debates made him the natural heir to Townshend when he suddenly died on 4 September. Townshend himself is reputed to have made this comment on North not long before: 'See that great, heavy, booby-looking, seeming changeling. You may believe me when I assure you as a fact that if anything should happen to me, he will succeed to my place, and very shortly after come to be First Commissioner of the Treasury.' Another story of the time made the same point. Grenville was out walking with a friend who commented, 'I wonder what he is getting by heart, I am sure it cannot be anything of his own', when they met North rehearsing a speech. 'You are mistaken,' replied Grenville, 'North is a man of great promise and high qualifications, and if he does not relax his political pursuits he is very likely to be Prime Minister.'[42] These stories are so neat and prescient as to be suspect: but even if they are exaggerated or unfounded, their currency is testimony to the informed contemporary opinion that North at the age of thirty-five had a bright political future.

2

FROM CHANCELLOR OF
THE EXCHEQUER
TO PRIME MINISTER
1767–70

Lord North has taken the place of Chancellor of the Exchequer, and is esteemed a man of good abilities, though by no means of such brilliant talents as his predecessor. It is said, he understands the business of the finances very well, and it is thought will be inclined to frugality, and economy in the conduct of the revenue. He was with the Ministry in all the measures of last winter, but did not speak very often in the House; when he did, he was well heard, and has a dignity in his manner that gives weight to his sentiments, which were generally sensible, cool, and temperate. He was against the colonies in the affair of the Stamp Act, though not amongst the most violent. But if he continues in this station, we shall soon be able to form a much better estimate of his character than can be made upon any former scenes he has appeared in.

This was how Connecticut agent William Samuel Johnson brought to the notice of his colony the man whose name was soon to be universally known in America.[1] On Charles Townshend's death George III at once instructed Grafton to offer the Exchequer to Lord North. Grafton later recalled that 'the choice of this nobleman was particularly satisfactory to me, as I knew him to be a man of strict honour: and he was besides the person whom Lord Chatham desired to bring to that very post'. All the administration favoured the appointment; all the political world expected it. North was at Wroxton where his father was seriously ill, but he travelled to London to see Grafton and George III on 9 September. North then declined the post, but Grafton evidently shared the general expectation that he would change his mind, for he offered the Exchequer to Secretary at War Lord Barrington as a temporary expedient. Barrington, who had held the post for a year, 1761 to 1762, accepted with reluctance, informing the Duke that he had urged Newcastle even at that time to appoint North instead of himself: 'I have long thought him the man in England best fitted for that employment.' Grafton then left London for his country home at Euston: but on the way he received a letter from North, dated 10 September at Wroxton, announcing that he was now willing to accept the office if Grafton was in 'real difficulty' about the appointment; and the Duke gave him no chance to change his mind again. The reason North gave was his father's sudden recovery of health. George III believed that Halifax had been instrumental in securing Guilford's consent to the appointment, and North may have been awaiting his father's approval. But his correspondence does reveal genuine diffidence about acceptance of a post which would involve him in considerable work in the public eye, exposing him to criticism from experts like Grenville: and it was a move that offered no financial reward; the salary of £2,500 may even have been lower than the one he was enjoying at the Pay Office.[2]

Grafton soon found that North was a great improvement on his predecessor at the Exchequer, later making this note in his memoirs: 'At the Treasury his talents for business in finance were eminently superior to anything we had seen in Mr C. Townshend.' The mere news of his appointment increased the confidence of City financiers in the government. North brought the experience of six years at the Treasury, great competence, and the asset of reliability notably lacking in Townshend. Grafton could safely leave Treasury business in his hands, and did so. After having attended the Treasury Board regularly when Townshend was at the Exchequer, the Duke seldom appeared there from early in 1768; and North even conducted formal departmental business with the King.[3]

What might appear a consequence of North's appointment was the regular summons to cabinet he now received. But Townshend had been only the first Chancellor of the Exchequer to attend as of right; and North's claim to a cabinet seat was his role as ministerial spokesman in the Commons, not his post as Chancellor of the Exchequer. He told his father that Grafton had assured him that

> he understood it to be the King's intention that I should always be summoned and considered a member of the cabinet. I have not the vanity to imagine that my advice can be of any consequence . . . but it will be very difficult for me to act in concert with the cabinet and promote their plans in Parliament, unless I am present at the meetings at which they are formed.[4]

It was evidently the assumption that North would now be the administration's voice in the Commons, and he succeeded Conway as Leader of the House in January 1768.

North's first session as Leader of the House was a quiet one, and little evidence has survived on his performance. He bore responsibility for a Bill to continue the limitation of East India Company dividends; and, according to Edmund Burke, 'no man ever got such a drubbing as Lord North' on the third reading on 25 January 1768. On 17 February North led the ministerial attack on the Nullum Tempus Bill: but this popular measure to impose a sixty-year limit on claims by the Crown to royal lands was defeated by only twenty votes, and the opposition was rightly confident of success the next session.[5] This was an inauspicious start: but within a year or so North was master of the Commons, as a result of the second Wilkes case of the Middlesex elections, one of the major political controversies of the century. Grafton subsequently recalled that 'if Lord North did not rise in popularity, without doors, he rose greatly in the estimation of those who were the best judges of distinguished Parliamentary abilities'.[6]

John Wilkes, sentenced and outlawed in 1764 in the *North Briton* case, returned to Britain in February 1768, in time for the general election of the next month. The ministry did not order his arrest, and after an unsuccessful candidature in London he was elected M.P. for Middlesex. This was a direct challenge to the government, for the return of an outlaw to Parliament was illegal. The political time-bomb exploded under an administration already rent by internal discord. In December 1767 the Bedford faction had joined the ministry, with Lord Gower becoming Lord President of the Council and Lord Weymouth replacing Conway as Secretary of State for the North. The problem posed by the accession to office of a group whose political line on America and other matters had been so markedly different from that of the Chathamites was made more difficult by two existing points of weakness: the general distrust of Shelburne by his colleagues, and the lack of firm leadership from Grafton, over whom hung still the shadow of Chatham's potential return. North had no personal connexion with either Bedfordites or Chathamites, but he sided with the former in favouring strong action on Wilkes. As Leader of the Commons he summoned a meeting on the subject of the most important administration supporters in the House, on 25 April; and George III sent him this letter beforehand:[7]

Though entirely confiding in your attachment to my person, as well as in your hatred of every lawless proceeding, yet I think it highly proper to apprise you that the expulsion of Mr Wilkes appears to be very essential and must be effected; and that I make no doubt when you lay this affair with your usual precision before the meeting of the gentlemen of the House of Commons this evening it will meet with the required unanimity and vigour.

The King could and did make his views known, but he did not dictate policy. The administration had not decided what to do before the new Parliament met on 10 May, and North was not permitted to give any official lead. The Chathamite part of the ministry had managed to postpone any initiative, not merely on grounds of caution and moderation but also because the legal position was not clear. Wilkes had appealed against his outlawry and though he had surrendered himself into custody had not yet been sentenced. It was theoretically possible that there would be no reason to take action against him.

The day Parliament met was marked by a number of riots, notably one in St George's Fields outside the prison where Wilkes was being held. Soldiers were summoned to disperse the mob, and several deaths resulted in what was soon to be dubbed a 'massacre'. The reaction at Westminster was in favour of stronger measures, and there followed a revolt in the government ranks against the seeming pusillanimity of official policy. North held another meeting of ministerial supporters in the Commons on 12 May, when most speakers urged the immediate expulsion of Wilkes, a move opposed only by the Chathamites present.[8] Before Parliament adjourned for the summer North had made public his own sympathy with the hard-liners. On 16 May he supported a motion by Lord Barrington that the King should be empowered to call out the militia to deal with rioters, an implicit condemnation of official weakness: and two days later North gave tacit approval to a motion by the young hothead Henry Luttrell asking why the law had not been enforced against outlaw Wilkes, even though in his capacity as Leader of the House he killed it by an adjournment motion.[9]

Before the Middlesex election case became a crisis Chatham had resigned. This event was precipitated by the increasing alienation of Shelburne from his colleagues. Already he had been deprived of responsibility for the colonies by the creation of a new Secretaryship of State for America in January 1768, in the person of Lord Hillsborough: and the ensuing months saw a series of disputes, the most important of which concerned the sale of Corsica by Genoa to France in May. Grafton, sceptical of the argument that this change threatened Britain's naval position in the Mediterranean, overruled Shelburne's attempt to make an international issue of it. By September George III and Grafton had decided to remove Shelburne, but postponed this step through fear that it might cause the resignation of Chatham himself. There followed an ironic sequence of events. Chatham resigned on 12 October under a misapprehension that Shelburne had already been dismissed. When, on learning the truth, he changed his pretext to health reasons, all the scruples of his followers were removed and only Shelburne resigned from the cabinet with his chief. Grafton, Lord Chancellor Camden, and the others appointed by Chatham in 1766 remained in office.

It was therefore the Grafton ministry, shed of the incubus of Chatham's formal membership and potential return, that faced the problem of the Middlesex election. The legal position of Wilkes was resolved in June, when his outlawry was reversed but he was sentenced to twenty-two months in prison for his previous libels. Even now the Grafton administration was reluctant to adopt the logical course of expulsion. It was Wilkes, fearful of a decline into penniless obscurity, who forced the issue. Early in November he announced his intention of petitioning for a redress of grievances and then turned down two offers from Grafton of the compromise that if he would drop the petition no action would be taken against him in Parliament. This obduracy hardened opinion within the ministry, as North, himself an advocate of firm action, reported with satisfaction to his father on 14 November:[10]

The administration was well inclined to do nothing upon the subject of Mr Wilkes, but he has resolved to force his cause upon them . . . by presenting a petition . . . We shall probably have much tumult, noise and clamour in this business, but I do not see how it can end without his expulsion. He has brought it on himself, and must answer for the consequences.

North was premature, for Grafton was still trying to avoid that denouement. Moderate hopes of an alternative solution were finally shattered by a new provocation from Wilkes in the *St James's Chronicle* of 10 December. He published in that newspaper a letter written by Secretary of State Weymouth on 17 April that had advocated riot control by the use of troops; and in a preface claimed it as proof that 'the horrid massacre' in St George's Fields on 10 May had been planned by the ministry. This libel infuriated Grafton, who now accepted the policy of expulsion long urged by the Bedfordites, North and the King. On 15 December the Duke carried a resolution in the Lords that the comment by Wilkes was 'an insolent scandalous and seditious libel'. The next day North moved that the Commons should agree with this resolution, but met opposition from his own side of the House. Conway urged that Wilkes should be present, and Solicitor-General John Dunning, a follower of Shelburne, argued that Wilkes should be heard before the Commons passed judgement. Grafton later recalled that this behaviour 'offended Lord North much more than it need have done: he complained to me next day most bitterly'. Lord Chancellor Camden declared that Dunning had acted correctly as a lawyer, and Grafton told North this: but 'the prejudice of Lord North against Mr Dunning was not removed by this explanation of ours, nor could he be brought to treat him with that confidence which the situation of the other had a right to expect from the minister of the House of Commons'.[11] North was not being petty. He saw the behaviour of Wilkes as both an attack on the constitution and as a catalyst of violent challenge to law and order. Hence his anger with office-holders like Conway and Dunning who failed to give him what he thought to be proper support in Parliament.

It became apparent after the Christmas recess that the mood of the Commons was hostile to Wilkes. On 27 January 1769 North won a majority of 278 to 131 for a motion restricting consideration of Wilkes's petition to two specific points. These were allegations that before his trial in 1764 Lord Chief Justice Mansfield had altered legal records and that the then Solicitor to the Treasury had bribed a witness. These were matters on which there need not be any general debate. By 1 February the House had disposed of the petition and could concern itself with the issue of expulsion.[12]

In a real sense North owed his rise to power to John Wilkes. The *North Briton* case had brought him to prominence in the Commons.

Now the Middlesex elections case established his dominance of the House and won him the admiration and gratitude of the King, who had already told North that he attributed the large majority on 27 January 'principally to the ability shown by you both in planning the measure and in the execution of it'.[13] North did not perform the same role on the two occasions. In 1763 he acted as the foremost spokesman of administration policy, the member who proposed and argued for the government resolutions. In 1769 North was Leader of the House, and his duties were more complex. He did not now move the resolutions against Wilkes himself: but he was the most frequent speaker in debate on the government side, and the most effective one. He spoke not only with logical exposition of the constitutional case against Wilkes but also with fire in his belly, displaying righteous indignation and spontaneous anger. In addition to this active role in the Commons North was responsible for the management of the whole campaign. Resolutions were drafted and arguments devised to embrace as wide a spectrum of opinion as possible and to arouse every conceivable prejudice. Tactics were rehearsed with colleagues and supporters before debates, and the talent at the ministry's disposal deployed to best advantage. North had able assistants in his task: procedural expert Jeremiah Dyson in the forming of motions, a useful team of government lawyers in debate, and Treasury officials competent in the organization of the administration's voters. But it was he who deservedly received credit for the success of the campaign against Wilkes, one that extended over several months and involved the defection of many supporters uneasy at the course of events.

On 3 February the expulsion of Wilkes was proposed by Secretary at War Lord Barrington. His motion was a composite one, citing two seditious and three obscene libels by Wilkes and also his current imprisonment, a mode of proceeding calculated to obtain the maximum support and denounced by opposition speakers as unfair. The debate was long and well argued, an occasion marked by many fine speeches that did credit to the House of Commons. North himself rose late, to pour scorn on the perils that Edmund Burke had suggested were implicit in such a precedent: 'The honourable gentleman is always terrifying himself when there is no danger, and puts me in mind of the fable of the shepherd's boy who was always crying out that the wolf was coming.' Wilkes had brought his fate on himself and was quite unrepentant about his behaviour. 'After what has taken place, I consider his expulsion to be necessary for the honour of the House, and the tranquility of the kingdom.' Wilkes was being treated according to precedent and in the same way that anyone else would have been. The expulsion was carried by 219 to 137.[14]

This event was not the 'very proper end of this irksome affair' that George III envisaged.[15] The King, and perhaps also his ministers, did not anticipate what would happen next. Wilkes was re-elected for Middlesex without opposition on 16 February. The administration acted the next day in the Commons when Lord Strange moved that Wilkes was 'incapable of being elected a member to serve in this present Parliament', asserting that it was 'a law of Parliament' that no M.P. could sit in the same House after expulsion. The debate grew warm, and North called James Townshend to order for suggesting that the county of Middlesex should petition for the dissolution of Parliament. That would be a breach of privilege, he declared. North had allowed his anger to get the better of him, and Yorkshire M.P. Sir George Savile asked for an explanation of this remark. North was heckled as he made the unconvincing reply that he had issued not a threat but a warning that M.P.s might be incensed by such petitions: 'People must take care how they push the forbearance of Parliament.' North also spoke avowedly in his capacity as Leader of the House – 'in the situation I stand' was his phrase – to answer an accusation by Edmund Burke that the administration was making 'the law of Parliament' from one or two precedents. 'Is it not also the law of reason and of common sense?' North asked, that expulsion must imply exclusion from the same Parliament. In his opinion Wilkes ought to be prevented from sitting in that Parliament 'on account of his crimes'. The administration resolution was carried by 235 votes to 89, and the second Middlesex election was then declared void.[16]

On 16 March Wilkes was elected a third time for Middlesex, again without an opponent venturing to stand against him. The next day Richard Rigby, now Paymaster-General, moved that the election was void. Opposition spokesmen did little more than denounce the absurdity of monthly elections for Middlesex and assert that the chief consequence of the administration's policy was to keep Wilkes in the public eye. North correctly forecast that the House would not even vote on the subject this time, and jovially said that he was glad to hear of the money being raised by the Bill of Rights Society to support Wilkes: 'I had as lief the money should be in his pocket as in that of his subscribers.' He ended with a clear hint as to how the ministry would get out of the impasse: 'If ever this question should again come before us, I shall deem that man the true member for the county of Middlesex, who shall have a majority of legal votes.'[17]

This declaration produced a volunteer, the Colonel Henry Luttrell who had raised the subject of the first Middlesex election in May 1768. He now resigned the seat he held for Bossiney and stood against Wilkes after a promise that the administration would secure his return. At the election on 13 April he obtained 296 votes as against 1,143 for Wilkes, who was returned a fourth time for Middlesex. The next day the election of Wilkes was declared void without discussion or voting; but a long and heated debate took place the following day, 15 April, over a motion by George Onslow, a junior Lord of the Treasury, that Luttrell ought to have been returned. Once again North rose to reply to Burke, contending that 'the freeholders who polled for Mr Wilkes, in my opinion, threw away their votes'. The House of Commons had defended its control over its membership against the Crown and against the House of Lords. Was it to be surrendered to 1,100 freeholders ? 'Though the public mind may at the present moment be in a disturbed state, let not the Parliament fall into contempt: let not liberty be established upon the ruin of law.' Uneasiness among administration supporters at the decision to seat Luttrell was reflected in the fall of the ministerial majority to fifty-four, 197 votes to 143.[18] And the following morning George III wrote to boost North's morale:[19]

The House of Commons having in so spirited a manner felt what they owe to their own privileges as well as to the good order of this country and metropolis, gives me great satisfaction, and must greatly tend to destroy that outrageous licentiousness that has been so successfully raised by wicked and disappointed men; but whilst I commend this, I cannot omit expressing my thorough conviction that this was chiefly owing to the spirit and good conduct you have shown during the whole of this unpleasant business.

North was in 'low spirits' at the time; it was probably at royal instigation that Secretary of the Treasury Thomas Bradshaw had a long conversation with him on 15 April, and persuaded North to 'continue to bear the unpleasant situation he is in, rather than be the cause of a general change in Your Majesty's administration', so Lord Hillsborough reported to George III at second-hand.[20] Already the key figure in the ministry, North was feeling the effect of a session difficult both as Leader of the House and as Chancellor of the Exchequer. The Middlesex election had merely been the most spectacular of the parliamentary problems facing the administration in 1769. Some subjects had proved only a temporary embarrassment. The revived Nullum Tempus Bill was accepted by the ministry with little resistance, after a defeat by 205 votes to 124 in a test of feeling in the House on 24 February; and North was prudent enough not to criticize the popular measure himself in debate.[21] On other issues he was perforce of necessity in the thick of the battle.

One was the Civil List Debt. On 28 February North presented to the Commons a royal message stating that the King had incurred a debt of over £500,000: and, describing himself as 'the last and the least of the Chancellors of the Exchequer' concerned, he promptly agreed to an opposition demand for accounts. This concession was not enough to avert criticism. Radical M.P. William Beckford asked whether the money was to be voted before the accounts were examined, and dull William Dowdeswell, Chancellor of the Exchequer under Rockingham, suggested that the accounts of each ministry should be distinguished. The sharper North pounced to turn this point against the opposition, agreeing that the responsibility must be divided among all the administrations of the reign. He then argued that it was a matter quite distinct from the question of paying the King's debts, since justice must be done to the creditors of the Crown. In any case the accounts could not be produced immediately, and it was parliamentary practice to consider such royal messages as soon as possible. The opposition did not accept this, and before the Committee of Supply met the next day Dowdeswell proposed that it should first consider the causes of the debt. North complained that his words had been 'taken up, noted down, repeated, and brought again to me', and defended the method of proceeding on ground of precedent. But he broke the rules of parliamentary debate by deliberate reference to the King: George III, he said, had been generous, 'but he will be the last man in the world to remind his people of what he has done for them'. Dowdeswell's motion was defeated by 248 votes to 135. North then proposed that £513,000 should be voted to discharge the Civil List arrears. He explained that the debt had arisen from a variety of causes: the funeral of George II, the coronation of George III, the King's marriage and his family commitments, which now cost £140,000 a year. Other less personal items were the cost of pensions to past servants of the Crown, the reduction or abolition of which would be impossible; and the expense of the diplomatic service, which cost over £100,000 and to cut which would mean a loss of international prestige. The resolution was approved without debate, but on the following day, 2 March, Dowdeswell attacked North for unconstitutional use of the King's name in debate, and Grenville argued that retrenchment should accompany payment of the debt so that one would not occur again. North wisely refused to make any promises.[22]

In the 1769 session North was also confronted by two of the long-term problems that were to beset him throughout his own administration – India and America. The ministry had been negotiating an agreement with the East India Company since August 1768, and early in 1769 completed it after hard bargaining and pressure on the Company. The central feature of a complex settlement, designed to last five years, was that the Company would continue to pay £400,000 a year to the government, but the dividend limit was raised to a maximum of 12½ per cent. The plan was presented in the misleading form of an offer from the Company, as a petition submitted to the House of Commons on 15 February: but the real battle had been fought at India House, where the ministry had coerced the Company into acceptance by the threat of referring the whole subject of India to Parliament. North had little difficulty in obtaining the consent of the House of Commons to the plan on 27 February, when he portrayed it as a postponement of 'the claim of the public' for five years more. He himself thought that the Indian territories belonged of right to the Crown, but he preferred 'the method of bargain and amicable agreement to a Parliamentary inquiry and legislative decision'.[23]

The American question could not be put off so easily. By the midsummer of 1768 abundant evidence had come of colonial resistance to the Townshend duties: everywhere there seemed to be constitutional declarations that Parliament had no right to tax America at all, trade boycotts were again being instituted, and in Boston there had once more been violence. The government sent four regiments of soldiers to that turbulent town, and quiet ensued there by the autumn. But the political problem remained, and its consideration was made more difficult by a cabinet split on policy. The Chathamite part of the ministry was reluctant to embark on the coercion demanded by their colleagues, among them North, who made his own views clear during the debate of 8 November 1768 on the Address. Connecticut agent Johnson reported home that North had declared that he would not think of repealing the Townshend duties 'until he saw America prostrate at his feet'.[24] On 7 December North took a firm stand on Parliament's right of taxation when debating a Pennsylvania petition that denied it: 'I think no line can ever be drawn. You must possess the whole of your authority, or no part of it.' Later that day North opposed a motion by Beckford calling for American papers. He said that no one could be more anxious than himself to see the restoration of harmony between Britain and the colonies, but the cause of the trouble was already known. It was 'the false apprehensions, on the part of the Americans, of their rights'. He would oppose another surrender, and, while disclaiming 'harsh measures', concluded with this declaration: 'I am against the repeal of the act, it would spread an alarm, as if we did it from fear, from want of spirit.'[25]

North might hold and express strong views on America, but he was not the man who decided policy. Grafton put forward a face-saving formula of parliamentary resolutions that condemned the American resistance and commended the government for sending soldiers but proposed no action except the possible transfer, if necessary, of treason trials from the colonies to Britain. The administration was thereupon attacked in Parliament both for being too severe, in the deployment of troops and the possible trials procedure, and for not doing enough: for the silent non-enforcement of the Townshend Acts would continue. In the main Commons debate of 26 January 1769 Grenville ridiculed the resolutions as trite and scorned the remedy of transferring trials to Britain as 'waste paper', forecasting quite correctly that the idea would never be implemented. North had the difficult task of attempting to strike a balance: 'Let us maintain our ground there; but, at the same time, do not let us unnecessarily irritate the people. Do not let there be fresh grounds of dispute. Let us not give way; and especially let us not give way to force.' For most of his speech he was concerned to defend government policy against the charge of weakness. The presence of soldiers in Boston had quelled the riots and restored the authority of the Crown, he said. These resolutions did not prevent further action, and the mere retention of the Townshend duties would have an effect on America, since their repeal had been widely expected there.[26]

North's debating skill could not conceal the failure of the administration to devise an American policy. The split within the ministry was made apparent by the Commons debate of 19 April on a motion by former Massachusetts governor Thomas Pownall for a Committee on the 1767 Revenue Act. Conway suggested that the Revenue Act should be taken into consideration the next session. North at once rose to disagree, arguing that such a declaration would be a virtual promise of repeal.[27] This public difference of opinion anticipated that in the important cabinet meeting of 1 May on America. Grafton there proposed that all the Townshend duties should be repealed the next session, being supported by Conway, Camden and Granby, all men appointed by Chatham. But these four were overruled by the other five present, who decided to retain the tea duty, while agreeing to repeal the other duties on the commercial ground that they were taxes on British products.[28] One of the five was North, who had already declared in the debate of 19 April: 'I see nothing uncommercial in making the Americans pay a duty upon tea.' The ensuing American crisis was to develop from this crucial decision of the Grafton cabinet on the tea duty. North, when minister, was to be confronted with the consequences of his own personal attitude to America.

It had now become clear that the Chathamite part of the administration had lost control of policy, and Grafton had already begun to contemplate resignation even before events later in 1769 threatened to bring about the fall of his administration.[29] The opposition used the parliamentary recess to launch a petitioning campaign throughout the country on the subject of the Middlesex election, in order to convey the impression of widespread popular discontent. The aim was to break the nerve of a ministry already shaken by parliamentary pressure, and the attack was assisted at coffee-house level by the vitriolic attacks on members of the government by the anonymous Junius letters in the *Public Advertiser*.

All the omens pointed to a difficult winter for the Grafton administration. By September there was a working alliance between Grenville and Rockingham, and every prospect that they would be joined by Chatham, who had recovered from his long illness a few months earlier. Instead of supporting the administration he had created three years before he was critical of its policy on Wilkes and India. Chatham's return to active politics threatened to have a divisive effect on the ministry. By the end of November it was clear the cabinet would lose Granby. Lord Chancellor Camden now made no secret of his hostility to the official policy on the Middlesex elections, and by December Grafton had acquiesced in the King's insistence that he would have to be dismissed. George III was indeed already anticipating the possibility that the Duke himself might resign. On 20 December he sent this summons to North: 'I wish to see you about eight this evening.' Five days later North commented to his father that 'my pride . . . has by the late offer been gratified to the utmost of its wish'. The inference is that the King had asked North whether he would accept the Treasury in the event of a vacancy.[30]

The stage was set for North's promotion to Prime Minister; but Grafton's resignation was by no means inevitable at the turn of the year. It seemed at first as if the opposition attack would fail. 179 M.P.s attended the government eve-of-session meeting at the Cockpit on 8 January, as against 80 at a rival opposition gathering.

North made an excellent speech next day on the Address, denouncing the petitions as the work of factions; and the administration majority in the Commons was nearly a hundred: 254 to 158.[31] This triumph was a deception. The ministry had not yet faced a direct challenge, and the debates had revealed the public defection of Chathamites in both Houses. General lack of confidence in the administration was underlined by the difficulty in filling the dozen or so offices vacated by resignations, notably the Lord Chancellorship. The King's attempt to solve that problem only made the crisis worse. On 17 January he bullied Rockinghamite Charles Yorke into accepting the Great Seal; but Yorke died three days later, of ill-health worsened by worry over a decision that involved desertion of his political friends. The shock shattered the morale of Grafton, who like many contemporaries believed the death to be suicide. The next day the Duke told George III that he intended to resign, and the King sounded North again about the Treasury. An interview on 22 January was followed by a letter the next morning in which the King told North that he was sending his cabinet colleagues Weymouth and Gower to press acceptance of the Treasury:[32]

My own mind is more and more strengthened with the rightness of the measure that would prevent every other observation. You must easily see that if you do not accept I have no peer at present in my service that I could consent to place in the Duke of Grafton's employment. Whatever you may think do not take any decision unless it is the one of instantly accepting without a further conversation with me.

While North was hesitating Grafton began to reconsider his decision. On 25 January he entertained hopes that Attorney-General William De Grey might agree to become Lord Chancellor, and gave the King reason to think that he would carry on after all. When North called on George III to give his answer the King, suddenly faced with the prospect of two Premiers instead of none, tactfully put him off for a day. The delay was sufficient. That evening saw a stormy debate in the Commons. Dowdeswell put forward a motion that in election cases the House was bound to judge according to the law of the land, a general proposition impossible to reject and yet unacceptable to the administration in the context of the Middlesex election. The Treasury Bench was unable to devise any counter, for procedural expert Jeremiah Dyson, nursing a grievance over a delayed pension, had refused to attend. Government speakers had to filibuster until Dyson, after several requests, condescended to supply a suitable amendment for North to move, that the decision of 17 February 1769 had been 'agreeable to the said law'. This was carried by a majority of only forty-four votes, 224 to 180.[33] The debate left government supporters disheartened and opposition M.P.s jubilant. It seemed that one more push would topple the administration.

The threat of parliamentary defeat caused a petulant Grafton to decide finally on resignation after he knew of De Grey's refusal to accept the Great Seal. On 26 January he informed George III, who at once put pressure on North. After seeing him on 27 January the King was confident of North's eventual acquiescence, and the next day instructed Lord Barrington to urge North's immediate acceptance in case news of the offer leaked out beforehand. North thereupon took the Treasury, inheriting a ministry thought to be on the point of collapse even before Grafton's resignation. Premature disclosure of the change before North could contact potential supporters might well wreck all hopes of the administration's survival, and the secret was kept until 30 January. Meanwhile office-holders rallied to the Crown as North privately closeted them: here is the account given by one of them, Sir Gilbert Elliot, of his reaction to North's news:[34]

I told him that the resignation at this moment, so unexpected, and so near the late division, I thought might possibly cause great defection; for my own part, if the King was determined not to be forced, I would willingly give support to whatever might be the event; liked his being [in] the situation, but disliked the low state of the House.

North's future was balanced on a knife-edge. Defeat in the Commons would precipitate a constitutional crisis in which the King had failed to find a ministry acceptable to Parliament. 31 January was the day of battle. The opposition now knew that North himself was the first minister and sought his immediate defeat. North accepted the challenge and did not make the adjournment motion that was widely expected. In a Committee on the State of the Nation Dowdeswell put forward a motion about the Middlesex election even more difficult to counter than his previous one, the simple proposition 'that, by the law of the land and usage of Parliament, no person, eligible by common right, can be incapacitated by vote or resolution of this House, but by Act of Parliament only'. Opposition speakers claimed that such a proposition could not be negatived. North took the line that the motion was improper, for two reasons: it did not refer to current business and it contradicted a decision of the previous session. He therefore adopted the procedural device of moving that the Chairman should leave the Chair, so avoiding a direct vote on Dowdeswell's resolution. Later in the debate, answering personal attacks on himself, North made what was virtually a speech on accepting office. 'Lord North with great frankness and spirit, laid open his own situation, which, he said, he had not sought, but would not refuse, nor would he timidly shrink from his post': so reported Horace Walpole, who noted that North spoke 'with spirit but good-humour, and evidently had the advantage, though it was obvious how much weight the personal presence of a First Minister in the House of Commons carried with it'. Administration defeated opposition by 226 votes to 186, the majority of forty being larger than the most optimistic supporter of North had expected: and George III congratulated him on the 'very favourable auspice on your taking the lead in administration'.[35]

Contemporaries did not think the contest over, but the opposition failed to mount a continuous attack such as was to bring North down in 1782. The Middlesex election did not provide an issue comparable to the unsuccessful American war, and North was soon able to dismiss it with the jibe that opposition insistence on the subject reminded him of a man who had only one story to tell and insisted on bringing it into every conversation: and the opposition failed to develop a campaign against government 'influence' until too late. Valuable debating days were frittered away on matters of little consequence, and in this breathing-space North began to fill up vacant offices. The general willingness now of M.P.s to accept posts was a significant vote of confidence in North's prospects of survival. Not until 12 February did the opposition stage an important debate, on Dowdeswell's motion for the disfranchisement of revenue officers: this was a move calculated to appeal to independent opinion and an anticipation of the successful campaign for 'economical reform' mounted in the closing years of the North ministry. Dowdeswell argued that to allow such men to vote was equivalent to bribing electors by the £600,000 a year paid in salaries to revenue-collecting officials. North rose late in the debate, first to defend himself from this attack by Charles Cornwall: 'In the turn of the wheel, a dependent tool of one faction may attain a great office, and then tell you he is not ambitious.' North dealt briefly with this personal point, the charge 'that young men have been pushed forward into office. As far as that charge comes home to me, I confess it. I did not aspire to it. I was thrown into it.' He then turned the motion against the opposition. The mere fact that it had been made was an admission of their 'utter despair of effecting a change in the government'. It would never have been thought necessary if such upright and honourable gentlemen expected to replace his wicked and corrupt administration, a cogent line of argument for any M.P.s still hesitating which side to support. North then demanded some evidence as to why this change was now suddenly thought to be essential. In reply Grenville attacked North for his tactics in his previous major debate as minister, on 31 January: 'The noble lord has been but a few days in his present office. It is a melancholy introduction that he should, on the very first day, have suppressed a self-evident proposition, by a paltry motion for your leaving the Chair.' Grenville was especially angry because North had again put forward the same motion. This time he won by 263 votes to 188.[36] The rise in the administration majority from forty to seventy-five was apparently due to the tellers counting one ministerial bench twice:[37] but, whether or not an error occurred, news of the division greatly improved North's prospects of victory.

Soon the ministry began to win regularly by majorities of that size. Triumphs by sixty-nine and seventy-five votes on 16 February were followed by a majority of ninety-seven on 28 February, when North secured the rejection of a motion by Grenville for the previous year's Civil List accounts.[38] These successes were won in full houses of over 400 members. Attendances began to fall as the parliamentary threat to the administration ended, and by the Easter recess contemporaries realized that North was there to stay. 'Lord North bids fairer for making an able and good minister than any we have had a great while,' wrote Lord Barrington to the British envoy in Berlin on 24 April.[39]

3

PRIME MINISTER:
THE GOOD YEARS
1770–75

North had risen to power through Parliament:
yet although he enjoyed the personal goodwill of many private
friends and political associates he had become first minister without
a following of his own. This was an unusual path to 10 Downing
Street in an age of faction politics. Contemporaries accustomed to
seeing 'connections' in office therefore entertained unfounded suspicions of North's role. Some thought him only a front for the
Bedford House faction in the administration, one to be discarded as
soon as possible. Such an interpretation exaggerated the influence
and unity of the Bedford group: Gower did aspire to North's office,
and Weymouth was a man of ambition, but both lacked North's

advantages at Whitehall and Westminster; and their associates Sandwich and Rigby were soon inclined to hitch their wagon to North's star. Another fiction portrayed North as the instrument of Lord Bute, whose political hold over George III had in fact dissolved some years before and with whom North himself had never been on good terms: yet Junius fell back on this absurd accusation in his *Letter to Lord North* on 22 August 1770.

Later there developed the more enduring legend that North was merely a puppet Prime Minister while the King in reality ruled Britain himself. This is the so-called 'Whig interpretation of history' as applied to George III, the view that the King was determined to restore royal control of government by ruling through Parliament now that more direct methods were no longer possible after the defeat of the Crown in the seventeenth century. Little time need be spent on a contemporary and historiographical myth long since demolished by historians. George III did insist on his right to appoint ministers, but having done so he let them govern. Decision-making on policies came at the level of department and cabinet, and the approval of the sovereign was largely formal.[1] George III frequently informed ministers of his opinions, but that was as far as royal influence on policy went: Hillsborough told former Massachusetts governor Thomas Hutchinson in 1775 that the King 'will always leave his sentiments and conform to his ministers, though he will argue with them, and very sensibly; but if they adhere to their own opinion he will say, "Well: do you choose it should be so? Then let it be." '[2]

The balance of decision-making in eighteenth-century government fluctuated not between the sovereign and his ministers but between the Prime Minister and his colleagues. This is yet another modern charge against North, that he was not master of his cabinet. But the system of government that operated under North was more characteristic of the age than a domineering first minister. It was the usual practice for department heads to introduce appropriate business and devise policies; and for cabinet decisions on them to be collective and often compromise. During the previous decade Bute, Grenville and Grafton had all been overruled on policy within their own cabinets; and it is misleading to compare North only with such strong Prime Ministers as Sir Robert Walpole and the two Pitts. He was certainly prone to chronic indecision. In 1775 Charles Cornwall, then a Lord of the Treasury, told Thomas Hutchinson that he attributed 'the delays which attend business of all sorts, to Lord North's consulting so many persons, who are of very different opinions; and from this difference he remains undecided himself for some time, and after he appears decided, he is apt to change.' But Cornwall ended this character assessment with an important qualification: 'When forced to engage, he shows himself exceeding capable.' Most of the important measures of North's administration – on finance, India, Ireland, and America – were essentially the policies of the Prime Minister himself: and Hillsborough made the shrewd observation in 1775 that North 'in important affairs [was] not governed by others'.[3]

North was not merely Prime Minister. He was also Chancellor of the Exchequer and Leader of the House of Commons. The first of these posts as yet lacked the great importance it has later come to possess, and the second was unofficial: but they signified the two foundations of his political power. Finance was the most important part of government business, and North was fortunate in that experience and ability marked him out for success in that field. He excelled in both mastery and presentation of the nation's accounts. If debating skill had brought him to power, financial expertise helped him to retain office.

It is scarcely possible to exaggerate the great advantage North enjoyed of being an M.P. when all his possible rivals were peers. That is what made North indispensable to George III in 1770, and the situation did not change during his ministry. In this sense the duration of the administration depended on Guilford's life, for there was no one in the Commons to fulfil North's role if he left for the Lords. No natural successor emerged on the government side, and therefore throughout the American War continuous pressure on North to remain Prime Minister came from his colleagues and subordinates as well as from the King. Occasional schemes of replacing him were not seriously considered, except by a few men ambitious for themselves; and this attitude represented a frank assessment of political reality. Every stable ministry of the eighteenth century was headed by a commoner. The simple fact of a Prime Minister being in the Commons was such a great asset that one newspaper reported that Grafton had given the King that reason for his resignation:[4]

As he found the great strength of the increasing minority was in the Lower House, he thought it most natural as well as advisable, to nominate a Premier there, in the scene of action, as he found, by daily experience, that that was the fittest place for a Prime Minister, and that there was no doing anything without it, as in the cases of Walpole, Pelham and Pitt.

The combination of what would now be three separate posts involved an immense burden of work. There were regular calls on

North's time quite apart from the multitude of individual tasks, political, administrative, financial, associated with each of the offices he held. The cabinet met on average twice a week, and so did the Treasury Board. North was expected to attend both on every occasion, and he had to be in his place in the House of Commons every day during the parliamentary session from mid-afternoon until the House rose. Public business was always postponed to await his arrival; his absence was a newsworthy item in the press and portrayed by opposition M.P.s as a slight to the House. In 1776 North was reproached for a brief absence of ten minutes from a debate of fourteen hours, and made a reply sharpened by a sense of injustice:[5]

I may, Sir, be deficient in many respects, but I never imagined that a want of respect, diligence as a member, or attention to this House, would have swelled the long catalogue . . . I trust, however, that I shall have the justice done me, to allow that there is no member in this House longer keeps his place, I mean my place in Parliament, or attends with greater patience and resignation, the whole length of tedious debate, than I do.

North's regularity of attendance was more than mere form. The eternal vigilance of the minister was the price of his administration's safety in the Commons. North was the eye and ear of the government there, and, most important of all, its voice. That he was the official spokesman was the true significance of his position as Leader of the House. During North's first five sessions as Prime Minister he made about 800 speeches and interventions in debate: and it is probable that he spoke some 2,000 times in the Commons during the twelve years of his administration. When North himself did not actually move the government proposals on important subjects he was usually the leading administration speaker on them. Many of these major speeches lasted one hour and sometimes two, a length then deemed formidable and requiring the apology that North always provided. Equally important was North's part in the cut and thrust of debate, for he often rose several times a day to defend ministerial decisions. North particularly concerned himself to justify government legislation in both principle and detail. He made ninety-six speeches on the two bills concerning the East India Company in 1773, seventy-two speeches on the Quebec Bill in 1774, and he rose countless times on America throughout his administration. This parliamentary burden fell on North because of the lack of adequate debating support. From 1771 to 1775 he was the sole member of the cabinet in the Commons, the only one who could speak with the authority and responsibility of high office. Alongside him other government spokesmen were makeweight, however numerous they were and however well they argued the ministry's case. Amid a company of minor office-holders Lord North stood out as 'the Minister'.

North fulfilled the role admirably. His imperturbable good humour was a quality particularly appropriate alike to the circumstances of his accession to office and to the disasters of the American War. It was symbolized by his notorious propensity for sleeping in the House of Commons. This habit had begun early, for during the debate of 22 November 1770 Barré made this comment: 'Was there ever, Sir, a minister that slept so much in Parliament? I have seen him taking his doze and his nap, while another gentleman has been taking notes for him.'[6] He had fallen asleep earlier that year when George Grenville was speaking about the state of the national finances. Treasury Secretary John Robinson nudged North just as Grenville was saying, 'I shall draw the attention of the House to the revenue and expenditure of the country in 1689'; whereupon North convulsed the Commons by the loud comment, 'Zounds, you have wakened me near one hundred years too soon.'[7] Complaints about North's somnolence punctuate debates in the next decade, but such famous stories as his correction of Burke's Latin pronunciation and his audible murmur 'I wish to God I were' suggest that he was sometimes resting his weak eyes and not asleep as often as he seemed.[8]

To temperament North added technique. He never made the mistake of preparing formal orations, as one of his daughters recalled after his death: 'He reflected on the subject and the arrangement, and perhaps composed a few sentences of introduction and conclusion, but left the rest to the extempore language which should occur to him in the act of speaking.' Confirmation of North's method came in 1802 from the King, who said that North had told him he never spoke from notes, and remarked that even for his Budget speeches North arranged the materials in his head after studying the relevant papers over a weekend.[9] Many of his speeches were necessarily spontaneous, arising out of the course of debates. It was North's sharpness in this respect that made him so formidable in the Commons. He was adept at exaggeration, distortion and evasion of opponents' arguments.[10] More important than such debating skills was the clarity with which North expounded his views and policies to the House. Nor was he ever tiresomely verbose, commanding parliamentary respect and attention throughout his career. North contrived to be comprehensive as well as concise. Possessed of a prodigious memory, he not only outlined the government case but also often refuted every point made against it: but sometimes, especially if he had been dozing, his memory had to be reinforced by perusal of notes made by his subordinates.

North's presentation of his arguments to the Commons was greatly assisted by his wit. His humour was his own even if his notes were not, and as infuriating to some opponents as his sleepiness; Edmund Burke sourly commented in 1770 that 'it is not sufficient when the first minister shall make you laugh'.[11] What made North disarming was that his humour might be directed ostensibly against himself. He knew his physical appearance was faintly ludicrous, and played the role of buffoon. He often began with self-deprecation that subtly turned to mockery of his opponents. This type of humour does not readily come alive out of the context of the debate; but here is one example, North's ironic comment in 1774 on the function of the parliamentary opposition:

> In the House I am sure every indulgence, every degree of grati-
> tude, I think are due to those gentlemen who undertake the very
> difficult, the very painful, the very meritorious task of watching our
> Ministers; of reprehending them; of blaming and calling them daily
> to account; they, Sir, deserve the indulgence of this House.[12]

Not for North the savage sarcasm that gave offence. Even an inveterate opponent like the Younger Pitt was later to say that he had never heard any other speaker with the same 'lively good-humoured wit': and George III commented in 1801 that nobody then possessed 'that easy natural flow of genuine good-natured wit which distinguished Lord North and forced a smile from those against whom it was exercised'.[13] North's political opponents did not become his personal enemies, and his easy-going nature made him the most approachable of men for M.P.s of all shades of opinion. No other Prime Minister can have been more universally liked in the House of Commons.

North's charm, wit and intelligence were also an asset in his ministerial task of patronage. The Treasury was the fount of most official favours as well as the most important department of business; but as Sir Robert Walpole had observed earlier in the century, there was never enough grass for the beasts to feed upon. North so mastered the art of refusal without offence that he became liable to misinterpretation, and on 17 February 1772 made this answer in the Commons to a complaint by Henry Seymour:[14]

It was the etiquette of the Minister, if he could not grant the favour asked of him, at least to send home the person refused in good humour. This was well understood by courtiers; but for such ignorant honest country gentlemen as the Honourable Member, he thought it right to explain, that, when he only nodded, or squeezed the hand, or did not absolutely promise, he always meant No; which produced a great and long laugh.

Applicants who in North's opinion were too importunate could never be soothed and took offence, as young Charles James Fox twice did in the early 1770s.[15] Undoubtedly, too, North was careless in dealing with the multitude of applications that he faced; and Horace Walpole thought that he gave frequent offence by failing even to reply.[16] But it was a greater weakness of North that he did not refuse as often as he should have done; and a common complaint of his friends that he granted too many favours to his opponents. Patronage became an administrative as well as a political problem. North kept 'books of recommendation', in which there were recorded daily the names of patrons and applicants for all manner of official appointments ranging from the customs service to the church. These volumes were indexed so that North could ascertain immediately the number and success of the requests from any sponsor or candidate. So great was the pressure of demand that North kept waiting lists, often with a backlog of several years: and, in the way of politicians, sometimes by-passed prior applications in special circumstances or under pressure from influential colleagues.[17]

North's qualities as man, minister and parliamentarian were to ensure him the goodwill of the House of Commons for over a decade. But general acceptance of North as Prime Minister did not mean endorsement by the House of all his policies and opinions. Charles Jenkinson said in 1775 that North had 'no assurance of the success of any measure until it is tried': but he realized that the corollary was that North could 'lose three or four questions in a session and not affect him'.[18] Jenkinson was speaking from experience. Almost every year North had been defeated in the Commons. Perhaps the most notable opposition success came in 1770 with the passage of George Grenville's Election Bill, which transferred the trial of disputed election cases from the House to Committees of members chosen by ballot. The measure was popular with independent members as a blow at government influence, and disliked for the same reason by many administration supporters, who on 30 March attempted to kill the proposal by postponing it for two months. North himself took a more moderate line than his followers, suggesting that this move should be interpreted literally, not as a rejection but as giving time for further consideration. North's argument failed to convince the House, the postponement was rejected by 185 votes to 123, and the bill became law that session.[19]

Four years later, on 25 February 1774, North's administration was defeated by the overwhelming margin of 250 votes to 122 over an opposition motion to make the Act perpetual. North was upset by this and briefly contemplated resignation until mollified by re-assurances from George III and his cabinet colleagues.[20]

Resignation threats were a recurrent feature of North's ministry. He was easily disturbed by parliamentary defeats and policy set-backs. A Commons man through and through, he attached more significance to the opinion of the House than did his sovereign and the aristocratic cabinet: and he had a lack of confidence in his own ability that he frequently expressed in public and private from the time he accepted the Exchequer in 1767. Historians, like his own contemporaries, have differed in opinion about the sincerity of North's pleas to be released from his ministerial treadmill. North's professed motive for retaining office was his sense of obligation to the King: yet on the rare occasions when George III showed signs of taking his resignation demands seriously North never pressed them. There is much truth in Hillsborough's comment on him in 1775: 'Nothing kept him from resigning but his love of money, and his father's desire that he would keep in till all his connections were provided for, and they were numerous.'[21] Office had not solved North's financial problems. His salaries and perquisites from the Treasury and Exchequer probably amounted to £7,000 a year; but John Robinson informed the King in 1777 that North had told him that his expenses had greatly exceeded his income since he had taken the Treasury, and his personal debts in that year amounted to nearly £18,000;[22] while Lord Guilford undoubtedly pressured him to do his duty by his family. He himself in 1773 at last obtained the court office he had so long coveted, becoming Treasurer to the Queen at the age of sixty-nine. Brownlow North advanced steadily up the clerical ladder of promotion: Dean of Canterbury in 1770, he became Bishop of Lichfield at the age of thirty next year, being subsequently translated in 1774 to Worcester and in 1781 to Winchester, one of the most lucrative sees in England. North also placed many other relatives and personal friends in public employments. Despite all his disclaimers, he usually behaved as if he enjoyed the power, prestige and perquisites of being Prime Minister.

Whether North would stay rather than whether he would survive soon became the chief political question for many of his contemporaries. Within a year or so of becoming Prime Minister he was firmly in the saddle, having established a pre-eminence in the cabinet and a close personal relationship with the King to reinforce a position in the Commons that became stronger each year that passed. For the parliamentary opposition simply fell to pieces in 1770 after North's initial success. Its connexion with the City of London was soon broken: already the extremist behaviour of the City radicals had been embarrassing and alienated the Westminster politicians; the death of Beckford in June severed Chatham's main link; and the release of John Wilkes from prison in April exacerbated the breach and produced a split within the City itself. In Parliament the opposition was weakened by deaths, desertions and divisions. The death of George Grenville in November was a great blow in itself and led to the defection of his group to the administration. The other two opposition factions of Chatham and Rockingham came to take differing views over an issue of great political interest, government prosecutions of press libels in 1770. Two matters gave cause for concern; the initiation of prosecutions by the Attorney-General himself and the evolution of a legal doctrine by Lord Chief Justice Mansfield and other judges that in libel cases the jury should decide only the fact of publication and not the technical question of libel. The Rockingham party drafted a bill to define the role of juries, but Chatham thought this step unnecessary and favoured a simple declaration in Parliament. This difference of opinion led to Rockinghamite Dowdeswell's bill being opposed by the Chathamites when it was finally introduced into the Commons on 7 March 1771. The administration let the opposition factions wrangle among themselves and then voted the bill down.[23] This opposition debacle came after defeat on the main issue of North's first year as Prime Minister, the Falkland Islands crisis.

This was the episode that enabled North to emerge as the dominant figure in the administration. Just as the Middlesex elections case had made him master of the Commons, so the Falkland Islands question put him at the head of the cabinet. North had inherited a cabinet in which Rochford, Weymouth and Hillsborough were Secretaries of State, Gower President of the Council and old Sir Edward Hawke First Lord of the Admiralty. It was abnormally small because in January 1770 Conway declined to attend any longer, and Grafton, Camden and Granby were not replaced on their resignations. Hillsborough was North's friend and political ally, and North's uncle Halifax took the Privy Seal in mid-February; but none of North's other colleagues had any attachment to him, and he was unable to find a Lord Chancellor. He put an end to this awkward situation by exploiting his advantages of being the government voice in the Commons and of possessing the King's ear when the ministry was confronted with the Falkland Islands question.[24]

This crisis seemed to bring to a head the danger that had faced Britain since the end of the Seven Years' War in 1763. Britain had settled for a foreign policy of 'splendid isolation', having found allies too difficult or too expensive to acquire: but she now faced the prospect of a war alone against the combined strength of the two Bourbon powers, France and Spain. The French minister Choiseul was planning a war of revenge on Britain, and the quarrel with Spain seemed to provide him with an excellent excuse. Spain had from the first objected to the British settlement made in 1766 on Falkland's Island, and on 9 June 1770 a Spanish force sent by the governor of Buenos Ayres compelled the garrison there to surrender. News of the incident reached Britain in mid-September. Already anticipation of trouble with Spain had led to pressure on Sir Edward Hawke to resign, and in August Sandwich had asked North for the Admiralty. North promised Sandwich his support for the post when it became vacant: 'I am too sensible of the importance of the situation of a First Lord of the Admiralty, and too well acquainted with your Lordship's abilities, not to be desirous of seeing you at the head of that department.'[25] Events were to show that North had made the right decision and secured a political ally; but Hawke was not willing to retire, and naval preparations were in a sorry state under his guidance during the next few months. At the end of December only thirty-six out of fifty-two ships of the line were ready, far fewer than the number available to Spain and her ally France.

When news of the incident reached London, Southern Secretary Weymouth at once demanded from Spain disavowal of the action and restoration of the *status quo*, without any salve to Spanish honour. King Charles III of Spain was prepared to return the island pending a settlement of the question but not to surrender Spanish claims to it implicitly or explicitly. Matters came to a deadlock, for neither country would make any move that might admit the other's claim or jeopardize its own. Lord North and the other ministers were at first confident that Spain would eventually give way, but they soon became uneasy about Weymouth's intransigence. He appeared to be intent on war, and was suspected to be aiming at power and prestige for himself and even at the replacement of North by Chatham. Gower therefore failed to support his fellow-Bedfordite, and Hillsborough and Rochford privately began to urge conciliation of Spain; but it was North who took the initiative.

North had always been anxious about Britain's naval weakness, and he knew that a war would ruin his long-term financial plans and might well bring down the ministry. He learnt from the French ambassador that war would be inevitable unless the deadlock was resolved, since Spain had no intention of yielding her claim. North was also aware of his colleagues' opinions and of George III's uneasiness about the prospect of war. At the end of November he intervened in the negotiations himself. Unable to make any formal concession, he nevertheless gave a private assurance to the French ambassador that Britain did not intend to keep the island and would in due course evacuate it if Spain gave way then. North had not obtained the prior sanction of his colleagues: but the cabinet promptly endorsed his proposal, with the condition that the promise of evacuation must remain secret. On 4 December all the cabinet except Weymouth decided to accept a Spanish declaration disavowing the seizure and promising to restore the British settlement. When the cabinet next met, on 7 December, Weymouth retaliated by proposing that the British ambassador should be withdrawn from Madrid. The cabinet postponed any decision on this matter, and turned down Weymouth's demand for a letter authorizing the East India Company to attack French settlements in India on any sign of military preparations there. Weymouth resigned three days later, on the ground that he had been constantly overruled in his own department.[26]

North had risen to the occasion in a manner befitting the head of the ministry. The cabinet vacancy was filled by Sandwich at Weymouth's own suggestion, so that Sandwich's place at the Post Office could be filled by Weymouth's brother Henry Thynne as a public sign that Weymouth had neither given offence nor gone into opposition. The more experienced Rochford moved to the Southern Department and Sandwich became Northern Secretary. The leadership of the administration was no longer in doubt. Sandwich was North's man, and the implicit challenge of a united Bedford group had come to an end. Gower and Rigby refused to follow Weymouth out of office, and the death of Bedford himself the next month accelerated the process of disintegration. North, moreover, had taken immediate advantage of the death of George Grenville on 13 November: within three days he told the King that he hoped to win over 'all Mr Grenville's friends', and before the end of the month he had an interview with Lord Suffolk, now the head of that faction.[27]

The incorporation of the Grenvillite group into the administration formed part of the ministerial reconstruction carried out by North at this time. One motive was to find a Lord Chancellor, and North achieved this in a legal reshuffle in January 1771. The undistinguished

Henry Bathurst proved willing to take the Great Seal with a peerage as Baron Apsley, Attorney-General De Grey became a Lord Chief Justice, Solicitor-General Edward Thurlow moved up to succeed him, and Grenvillite Alexander Wedderburn came in as Solicitor-General. The impending resignation of Hawke from the Admiralty was common knowledge and produced two candidates, Grafton and Sandwich. North promptly recommended Sandwich, and the King offered him the post on 11 January. Weymouth now hoped for the vacant Northern Department, but North wanted a man loyal to himself. He offered the post to Suffolk, who refused because he felt North was doing too little for other Grenvillites; then to his uncle Halifax, who was reluctant at his age to leave the comfortable post of Privy Seal; and finally to his step-brother Dartmouth, who declined because of his ties with the Rockingham group.[28] But Suffolk, after consulting his friends, reopened negotiations when Dartmouth refused, and within a few days concluded an arrangement providing places and pensions for various Grenvillites and by which he himself was to be Lord Privy Seal; for Halifax proved willing to move to the Northern Department after all. North now had a cabinet very much at his command. He had deliberately kept out the formidable Weymouth and had contrived also to exclude Grafton, perhaps fearing that the presence at cabinet of his recent predecessor would be an embarrassment. All but two of the cabinet were men personally loyal to North, and both of the others were sweetened by patronage: Rochford's brother obtained a lucrative sinecure, and Gower received the Garter vacated on Bedford's death. By the end of January North headed a united cabinet and a stable administration, well able to withstand parliamentary attacks on the Falkland Islands settlement.

Opposition M.P.s had already sought to make political capital out of the crisis. In the Commons debate on the Address on 13 November the administration was attacked for failing to make any military preparations before the seizure of the British settlement, and for blaming only the governor of Buenos Ayres instead of Spain. North replied that knowledge of Spanish claims had been no reason to expect an armed attack, and that it would be improper to accuse Spain for the act of one governor. He turned the tables on those who had raised the question of right: 'We should have done wrong to have suffered the question of right to have been entered into.'[29] The Address passed without amendment or vote: but on 22 November Dowdeswell moved for papers on Anglo–Spanish relations before the attack. The debate turned on whether the House had confidence in

Lord North, who took the line that while it was proper for Parliament to inquire into government policy the production of papers at that time would jeopardize negotiations with Spain, whereas postponement of them would not save ministers from any blame they might deserve. M.P. Charles Cocks told Lord Hardwicke that North 'did very well, and spoke with a wonderful superiority over his opponents, on the inconvenience and impropriety of such a motion, pending a negotiation of so delicate a nature. He debated with temper and firmness, and with better management of his voice than usual . . . What he said was received with extraordinary approbation.'[30] It was in vain that opposition speakers claimed that the papers called for were not concerned with the negotiations. Rigby said that only North could judge that, and 'everybody thinks it necessary to place some confidence in the first minister of the Crown'. Edmund Burke retorted that 'if ever there was a set of ministers who lost, totally lost, the hearts and confidence of the people, it is the present, through the whole course of their conduct'; but the House belied this claim by a majority of 225 to 101 in favour of postponing the motion for papers.[31]

The settlement with Spain was finalized and announced on 22 January, the official documents being submitted to Parliament on 25 January. The terms were those negotiated by North, for Spain had no choice but to accept them after Louis XV dismissed Choiseul in December and appealed to Charles III to avoid war. The opposition could find little to criticize in the formal agreement, for the verbal promise of future British evacuation was secret: but Dowdeswell moved for papers and claimed that Spain should have been made to contribute to British rearmament costs. By the time the papers were presented to the Commons on 4 February rumours of French intervention gave ground for an attack North found difficulty in parrying. In answer to repeated questioning he denied that France had been a mediator and refused to say whether she had interfered at all. Opposition members drew the obvious conclusion, Barré commenting: 'The noble lord will not deny it. If he had said "I will give you my honour it is not so", everybody would have believed him. The noble lord knew he could not do it.' North, embarrassed and angry, made this final retort to his tormentors: 'I am not to stand here, like a bear at a stake, to answer every question, and allow all the world to conclude, if I do not answer it, that I am guilty.' An Address asking the Crown for information on this subject was rejected by 173 votes to 57, a remarkable testimony to North's hold on the House in difficult circumstances.[32]

Nine days later, on 13 February, there took place a long, noisy and crowded debate on the Address of Thanks to the Crown for the settlement, the vote of confidence in ministerial policy. North rose late, and began with a characteristic touch of humour, saying that members of the opposition seemed to be so much better informed of the administration's intentions than he was that he doubted whether he should venture to discuss the matter. He portrayed the ministry's choice as having been between the agreement obtained and a war with both France and Spain, and no speaker had claimed that such a war would have been in Britain's interests. The question of right remained as before: but he played down the value of Falkland's Island and ended with this ambiguous remark: 'Let us not give up the right to Falkland's Island now. Let our conduct with regard to it be guided by the best interest of this country.' Edmund Burke got a noisy reception when he rose to reply to North at midnight, and complained of the contrast: 'I have not that authority, that rank, that power of language, those great abilities, which would entitle me to the attention of the House at this late hour.' Dunning seized on North's closing words to voice suspicion of a secret clause promising the abandonment of the island in the future, but the House paid no attention and voted the Address by 275 to 157.[33]*

North emerged from the episode a true Prime Minister, head of the cabinet with effective choice of his colleagues, and supreme in the House of Commons. His political success was completed by the establishment of a close personal friendship with the King. The first sign of this came in June 1771 when Halifax was dying. North privately informed George III and asked for his uncle's post of Ranger of Bushey Park, a mark of royal favour involving a house and salary. The King replied on 7 June, the day before Halifax died, expressing condolences and promising North the post: 'every opportunity of showing you the sincere regard I have for you is giving me the greatest pleasure'. George III gave further proof of his affection three days later by informing North that he intended to bestow on him the next available Garter 'with the greater pleasure' as North had not solicited it. North replied that he could only send the King 'his most sincere and most grateful acknowledgements', a response that 'much pleased' George III.[34] In June 1772 this honour, almost unique for a commoner,† was duly bestowed on North, who thereafter was often designated in parliamentary debate 'the noble lord in

---

* Falkland's Island was evacuated by Britain in 1774, but never occupied by Spain.

† Sir Robert Walpole in 1726 was the only precedent that century.

the blue ribbon'. George III had found in North a minister who could do the business of government at both Westminster and Whitehall and at the same time prove congenial in the royal Closet. The King, even when all too aware of North's faults, was never to part willingly with him.

On Halifax's death Suffolk accepted the Northern Secretaryship. The King then left North free to offer the Privy Seal to either Grafton or Weymouth. North chose Grafton, who accepted but refused to sit in the cabinet, doubtless to North's relief.[35] Having established his authority, North failed to exercise it in the way a Walpole or a Pitt would have done. Other ministers were allowed to take the lead even in matters not within their own departments, and there developed an intrigue against Hillsborough, North's chief prop in cabinet but a man increasingly isolated from his colleagues. It arose from a long-standing plan to establish a new colony of Vandalia in the Ohio Valley.[36] Although contrary to the policy of Hillsborough as American Secretary of preventing inland settlements, this scheme was favoured in 1771 by other members of the cabinet, including North. It was especially pushed by Gower and Rochford, who both had shares in the company planning the colony. As Hillsborough remained intransigent the whole manoeuvre developed wide political implications. Gower and Rochford intended to force the resignation of Hillsborough, and some contemporaries suspected that their real aim was to strike at North by the removal of his most loyal supporter from the cabinet. A few thought it a scheme to replace Hillsborough by Weymouth, others a plan by Rochford to abolish the American Secretaryship altogether and recover for his department the prestige and patronage lost at its creation four years earlier. When the Privy Council formally endorsed the Vandalia scheme in July 1772 Hillsborough threatened resignation, and North realized too late how seriously he regarded the affront. 'I find Lord North takes the thing much to heart and has certainly been actuated upon by Lord Hillsborough,' George III commented to Suffolk when deputing him to see North, whom the King blamed for 'natural good nature and love of indecision'. North tried without success to persuade Hillsborough to stay in office. He then approached Weymouth, expecting the refusal he duly received; for Weymouth did not regard the office as being of the same status as the other two Secretaryships. Next, at the King's command, he offered the American Secretaryship to Dartmouth without consulting his colleagues.[37] His letter was a personal appeal for support on the loss of a firm friend in Hillsborough, and his step-brother accepted after obtaining Rockinghamite consent.[38] This appointment more than balanced the loss to North of Hillsborough, and North's victory over the threat to his authority was further signified by the bestowal of an English earldom on Hillsborough, who retired temporarily off-stage, as Grafton and Weymouth had done before him, to join the reserve pool of potential ministers awaiting a recall to office, one that came for him seven years later.

This brief ministerial crisis of 1772 had shown North's inability to rule the cabinet with a strong hand. His success had been due less to his own efforts than to the support of the King. On the policy issue his dissident colleagues Gower and Rochford had had their way, although in fact their scheme was to be so delayed that it never came into operation, being overtaken by the Quebec Act of 1774. The significance of this omen of North's weakness lay some years in the future. Despite internal discord the cabinet was now to remain unchanged until the American War, and the period was one of considerable success for North.

In the 1770s the problems facing the British government were quite different from those of a generation earlier or a generation ahead. There was no challenge to the institutions of government from partisans of an old order or advocates of a new one, no longer any Jacobites and not yet any Jacobins: for the radicalism fathered by John Wilkes was merely an irritant and not a threat to the established system of government and society. What concerned contemporaries at the time North took office was not any fundamental constitutional danger but the chronic political instability of the previous decade, the constant change of ministries and ministers. Even before accepting the Treasury, North had voiced his awareness of the problem, in his speech of 2 March 1769 on the Civil List Debt. All the ministerial 'choppings and changes' of the 1760s, he said, had had 'a terrible effect upon public measures'.[39] His ministry was to provide a solution, offering stability and moderation. Stability came through an administration firmly based on the twin foundations of royal favour and parliamentary confidence. Every year he seemed to become more entrenched in power, and politicians soon ceased to think in terms of a possible change of ministry. Moderation embraced both resistance to change and reluctance to embark on 'new projects'. But if no new initiatives were taken on such subjects as Wilkes and America, they nevertheless forced themselves on North's attention.

In 1771 his ministry was drawn into the third Wilkes case, over the reporting of parliamentary debates in the press, by the attempt of some of his indignant supporters to stamp out this practice. North was soon giving ministerial support to their campaign against the newspaper printers, who took refuge behind the City of London's claim to exclusive jurisdiction within its boundaries: and he allowed himself to be pressurized by his backbenchers and provoked by the intransigence of the City radicals into taking a leading part in the clash between Commons and City. It was an angry North who on 25 March prompted the committal of Alderman Richard Oliver to the Tower. Lord Mayor Brass Crosby followed him two days later, after North's coach had been attacked and he himself hurt by an excited crowd outside the House of Commons. North had allowed his feelings to distort his judgement, and he had in any case been outmanoeuvred by Wilkes. The temporary imprisonment of the City officials gratified a parliamentary desire for vengeance but failed to prevent the permanent development of press reporting.[40]

North had been angered by the defiance of the House of Commons, and his concern for its prestige and power was the key to his political attitudes. Parliament must be defended from threats on all sides, from Crown, people and colonies. North deeply resented the contemporary charge that he was a Trojan Horse for the establishment of royal power within the House of Commons, and his view of the constitution was to be made manifest by his coalition with Charles James Fox in 1783 for the purpose of coercing the Crown by a Commons majority. Parliament for North was responsible only to itself, and he was always a strong opponent of the political reform movements that carried the implication of responsibility to a higher sovereign, the electorate. In the same way the British case against the American colonies was in his eyes the maintenance of Parliament's supremacy over all the King's dominions.*

The American situation had been temporarily defused, and in his first years as minister North seemed to have few problems of policy either at home or abroad. Within Britain there was political calm and economic prosperity: and in Europe the wisdom of Britain's policy of isolation was apparently confirmed by the successful outcome of the Falkland Islands crisis. But by the mid-eighteenth century Britain had acquired an empire, and it had to be governed. Contemporaries were slow to appreciate the complexity and difficulty of the problems that arose in North America, India and Ireland. Before he was obliged reluctantly to turn his attention overseas, North concerned himself with a subject closer to his heart and one more familiar to contemporaries – the financial state of the country and especially the National Debt.

* American policy is discussed in the next chapter.

North's mastery of finance was an important factor in his early political success. There was little need for new taxation in peacetime, for a comfortable surplus over and above the normal requirement of some £7,000,000 was derived from regular sources of supply. The famous land tax, an inflexible and inefficient charge based on fixed county quotas, yielded £500,000 for every shilling in the pound, and the rate was always three or four shillings. More productive and expanding sources of revenue were the customs and excise duties. There were also sundry luxury taxes, stamp duties and a window tax. Towards the end of each session, when most supplies and taxes had been voted, the Chancellor of the Exchequer would explain the balance of income and expenditure for the year and make his final proposals. North excelled in the clarity of his exposition of such matters, and Budget Day soon developed into a personal triumph for him.[41] Here is the comment made by Richard Rigby to the Duke of Bedford in 1769: 'In the four and twenty years that I have sat in Parliament, in very few of which I have missed that famous day of the session, I verily think I have never known any of his predecessors acquit themselves so much to the satisfaction of the House.' This was the occasion when, as Rigby reported to Bedford, North showed that he could match George Grenville, the acknowledged expert on finance in the Commons: 'Grenville laboured at a reply, and cavilled at the most immaterial parts of Lord North's observations . . . No part of Lord North's state of the nation hurt him more than to see there is a man in it and in the House of Commons who showed himself yesterday at least his equal in finances.'[42] North's triumph in the specialist field of his most formidable opponent was a landmark in his progress to mastery of the Commons. In 1770 Rigby reported that North had 'opened his budget in a most masterly manner', and after George Grenville's death that year he had no rival in the House. It became customary for the Commons to hear him in silence, and for M.P.s either to leave then or make a noise when opposition spokesmen attempted to reply. Any critics were at a disadvantage in that often the relevant information had only been presented to the House shortly beforehand, some of it the same day; and in 1774 opposition M.P. Isaac Barré commented: 'It is looked upon not only as unfashionable, but foolish to get up and dispute what is in the Budget.' Within a year or so, and certainly by 1771, North had developed the habit of completing his annual triumph by a political review of the year, a justification of ministerial policy to a crowded and attentive House.

By Budget Day North usually had little to offer, for both

expenditure and the main taxation measures would already have been voted. In 1770 he made a virtue of having no new proposals, and the chief interest of his peacetime finance centres on his astute use of the government lottery and his reduction of the National Debt, the capital burden of which at around £140,000,000 frightened many contemporaries. North found an annual lottery in existence as a device to encourage subscriptions to government loans. Such was the national gambling mania at the time that ticket-holders could resell their chance in the lottery at a substantial profit. In North's first year at the Exchequer he continued the lottery for its traditional purpose: each subscriber of £65 to a new issue of 3 per cent annuities was to have the option of buying three £10 lottery tickets out of a total of 60,000 tickets, all the money being distributed in prizes. The next year, 1769, North introduced a revenue lottery, intended solely to raise money and entirely divorced from the floating of a loan. He put the price of each ticket up to £13, and by keeping the total prize money at £600,000 obtained a profit of £180,000 for the Exchequer. North was able in this way to avoid levying any new taxes.

In 1770 North took further advantage of the popularity of the lottery by linking it with a stock conversion, having obtained the approval beforehand of some leading City financiers.[43] North's plan was to convert one eighth of the £20,000,000 4 per cent stock into 3 per cent stock, by offering two lottery tickets at £14 each to the holder of each £100 of stock so converted. Any of the 50,000 tickets unsold in this way could be bought by the general public; and with prize money limited to a total of £500,000 the Treasury would make a profit of £200,000 on the transaction. Opposition critics like Grenville and Dowdeswell said that all the 4 per cent stock should have been converted at once, an obviously impractical idea, and they claimed that the bargain was too good a one for the stock-holders, since they would be able to resell the tickets at a premium. North was defended from an unexpected quarter. Radical M.P. Beckford declared that 'there are fools that will give threepence, in order to play for twopence'; and he paid North the tribute of integrity: 'I believe the noble lord has no dirt sticking upon his hands.' In 1771 North again introduced a revenue lottery, this time of 50,000 tickets at £13 each, to yield a surplus of £200,000 after £450,000 had been paid in prize money. Although these terms were less generous than before, opposition spokesmen denounced the lottery as a new form of government influence. Charles Cornwall claimed that the tickets could be resold at a total premium of £150,000 by the first subscribers, who were all chosen by the ministry.

North denied this political charge at the time, and took care to remove the objection next year. For in 1772 he provided further evidence of his ingenuity by using the lottery to promote his debt-redemption schemes. North shared the concern of his contemporaries at the size of the National Debt, or professed to do so: certainly he was aware of the political kudos to be gained from an attempt to tackle the problem. In 1770 he announced the repayment of £1,500,000 during the previous year, and held out the prospect of similar repayments in future years: to which Grenville made the sour reply that increased customs duties were not a matter for congratulation. In 1771 North had to explain that the extra expenditure incurred during the war scare over the Falkland Islands question had not only obliged him to raise the land tax to 4s. but would also prevent him from paying off any more of the Debt. He expressed the hope that the next year he would be able to lower the land tax to 3s. again and begin a systematic reduction of the Debt; and in 1772 he achieved both of these aims. Later in the year North expounded his motives to Sandwich, head of the great spending department of the Admiralty:[44]

Should we, in time of profound peace, and without being able to assign any other cause than the great size of our establishments, let a year pass without discharging as much of the national debt as we have done this year, our credit would suffer exceedingly, our stocks might perhaps even fall upon it, and the nation be less in a condition to borrow if a loan should at any time be wanted than it is at present . . . This is the time, if ever there was a time, for a reasonable and judicious economy. It is our duty to avail ourselves of it, in order to get rid of some part of the burden of that debt, which lies so heavy upon us.

In his attack on the National Debt, North adopted a simpler and more flexible approach than the famous sinking-funds established by Sir Robert Walpole and the Younger Pitt. In contrast to their rigid allocation of an annual sum for this purpose North adopted the sounder approach of confining debt redemption to those years in which there was an actual Budget surplus. A second advantage of North's method was that he cancelled stock and so at once reduced the interest burden.

In 1772 North announced his intention of using a surplus of £1,300,000 to pay off some of the Debt. Since the market price of 3 per cent stock was around 87, repayment at the legal par of 100 to a favoured few would give them an unfair premium and expose him to justifiable criticism. North said that he would therefore invite holders to surrender stock voluntarily at 90, by offering the right to buy four lottery tickets at £12 10s. each for every £100 of stock surrendered. There would be 60,000 tickets and £600,000 in prize money. North explained that because of the linked debt redemption the Treasury profit of £150,000 would be less than in the previous year. He would be able to redeem £1,500,000 worth of the Debt in this way, and forecast that ten years of peace would make possible the repayment of £17,000,000 capital with the saving of £500,000 in interest. But in 1773 North had to inform M.P.s that the loan of £1,400,000 to the East India Company* would make impossible any reduction of the Debt that year. He also took the opportunity to drop the lottery after eight years, being afraid of killing the goose that laid the golden eggs. In 1774 North resumed his redemption scheme, planning to pay off £1,000,000 of the Debt by a Budget surplus of £730,000 and the inducement of a lottery. For every £100 of 3 per cent stock repaid at 88, slightly above the market price, he offered the holder six lottery tickets of £12 10s. in a lottery of 60,000 tickets providing £600,000 in prize money and yielding a profit of £150,000 to the Treasury. In 1775 North paid off another £1,000,000 of stock by offering an identical redemption price and lottery scheme. Thereafter the outbreak of the American War put an end to North's redemption schemes, and he returned to the more traditional use of the lottery as an inducement for the raising of government loans.

North's peacetime finance was an unspectacular success. In 1775 he informed the Commons that the redemption of that year would bring the total reduction of the National Debt since 1763 to £10,000,000, a fall from £136,000,000 to £126,000,000: while redemption and conversion would have cut the interest burden by £470,000 a year. North conceded that this might appear slow progress, but it had been achieved without new taxation and at a time of low public credit.[45] Certainly his ingenuity had made excellent use of the occasional surpluses with which he had been blessed. He was to be more severely tested during the American War.

Before that question came to dominate all others, North had been faced with other problems of empire, Ireland, India and Canada.† Constitutionally Ireland was not a colony but an independent kingdom with her own Parliament who had the same sovereign as Britain; but in reality she was ruled by a Lord-Lieutenant appointed by the British government. This viceroy faced a perennial problem

* See below pp. 63–6.
† Canada is discussed in the next chapter.

in the management of the Irish House of Commons, 300 M.P.s
elected on a narrow franchise that was almost a caricature of the
contemporary British electoral system, and one moreover that was
restricted to the Protestant minority. The management of the Irish
Commons was a matter requiring political skills as well as the liberal
disbursement of official patronage: but the Irish question was not of
the same dimension as the one that confronted later generations.
The Catholic population of Ireland, though a large majority, was
excluded from political power, and its existence was significant only
in so far as it constituted a latent threat to the ruling Protestant
oligarchy. The Irish problem facing the British government during
the North ministry arose not from the Catholic question but from the
demands of the Protestant Ascendancy for commercial and constitutional concessions.

In the mid-eighteenth century the economy of Ireland was subject
to many restrictions designed to prevent Irish competition with
British merchants and manufacturers: and Ireland lacked many of
the constitutional safeguards of liberty existing in Britain. Moreover, the legislative power of the Irish Parliament was restricted in
two ways: the so-called Poyning's Law of 1494 made necessary the
consent of the English Privy Council before legislation of the Irish
Parliament came into force and empowered the Council to initiate
bills itself; and a Declaratory Act of 1719 formally made Ireland
subject to Acts passed by the Westminster Parliament. By the reign
of George III these grievances were being taken up by a vocal group
of 'Patriots' in the Dublin Parliament, and some concessions had
already been made before North became Prime Minister, notably the
Octennial Act of 1768 which for the first time ensured that parliamentary elections in Ireland would be held at regular intervals.

The Irish situation had been exacerbated in the 1760s by an
important change in British policy. Before the reign of George III
effective control had been delegated by frequently non-resident
Lord-Lieutenants to 'Undertakers', Irish magnates who managed
the Dublin Parliament in return for a substantial share of patronage.
Increasing disenchantment in London with this system led to the appointment in 1767 of Lord Townshend as a resident Lord-Lieutenant
to recover direct power for the King's government. The result of
offending vested interests had been obstruction in the Dublin
Parliament as the Undertakers came to make common cause with
the Patriots. In November 1769 the Irish Parliament rejected a
finance measure sent over by the Privy Council in accordance with
Poyning's Law and then passed an identical bill itself, in order to

demonstrate that the grievance was constitutional and not financial. At the same time Lord Townshend was able to secure an increase in the Irish army from 12,000 to 15,000 men only by a royal promise that at least 12,000 men would always be kept in Ireland. Once these measures had been passed Townshend prorogued the Irish Parliament before it could proceed to other business.

Ireland fell within the departmental responsibility of the Secretary of State for the South, and North himself was not concerned with routine matters of administration: but he could not avoid becoming involved as Irish problems came before cabinet and Parliament with increasing frequency until within a decade his ministry seemed to be faced almost with a crisis comparable to that in America. North first had Ireland thrust on his attention when Lord Townshend's cavalier treatment of the Dublin Parliament was brought to the notice of the British House of Commons on 3 May 1770 by opposition M.P. Boyle Walsingham, a man closely connected with the former Undertakers. Walsingham moved for papers and denounced the Irish prorogation as both unconstitutional and detrimental to the interests of Ireland. North strongly defended Townshend. His action was not blameworthy but a 'signification of displeasure' at a deliberate defiance of Poyning's Law. No ministry, North said, could have ignored such a defiant breach of the constitution. Later opposition speakers accepted North's point that the administration could not have overlooked the matter, and merely attacked its handling by Townshend. North emerged with credit from his first Irish debate, and with a majority of 178 to 66.[46]

The North ministry was now committed to support an all-out attack on the Undertakers. 1770 saw the dismissal of many Irish officeholders who had voted against the administration, and the lavish use of patronage to win new support, the beginning of a policy that proved successful under both Townshend and his successor Lord Harcourt, Lord-Lieutenant from 1772 to 1776. Even the leading Patriot spokesman Henry Flood accepted office as a Vice-Treasurer of Ireland in 1775; this post, worth £3,500 a year, was usually reserved for a British politician but given to Flood with North's approval and possibly on his initiative. During these years only one subject brought Ireland to North's attention, a proposal in 1773 to levy a 10 per cent tax on rents paid to absentee landlords. North approved of the idea when Harcourt inquired about its reception in London, but Rockingham, the proprietor of large Irish estates, was soon busy organising public opposition to the measure. North at first stood his ground, saying that such a tax would afford relief to a distressed Ireland, but City interests and country squires swelled a rising tide of protest. On 29 October North finally admitted to Harcourt that the cabinet was in a quandary. The viceroy took the hint, and contrived to get North off the hook by bringing about the defeat of the tax in the Dublin Parliament a month later. North had learnt how difficult it would be to do anything for Ireland. There is reason to think from his letters and speeches that with a free hand he would have done more to meet Irish grievances before the Irish crisis at the end of the decade. On 12 March 1779 he made an indignant reply when Thomas Townshend warned him not to drive Ireland into rebellion. North portrayed himself as more of a friend to Ireland than any previous ministers had been. He had appointed native Irishmen to offices hitherto bestowed on Englishmen, and had refrained from the usual practice of increasing the Irish pension list as an easy form of British patronage. Later that year he twice listed in the Commons the economic benefits bestowed on Ireland by his administration.[47] North had acknowledged Ireland's grievances before changed political circumstances in both Britain and Ireland made it possible for him to give substantial concessions to meet them.

Like Ireland, but to a much greater extent, India was an imperial problem entangled in the web of contemporary British politics. It had already come to the attention of government and Parliament twice in the 1760s, and throughout that decade the East India Company had been a battleground of faction and intrigue. Ultimate authority within the Company lay in the Court of Proprietors, about 2,000 of whom held the voting qualification of £500 stock. Executive control was in the hands of twenty-four Directors elected annually by the Court. Such a constitution proved vulnerable to the machinations of men anxious to lay hands on the patronage implicit in the Company's novel possession of territories, and also of those simply wishing to engage in stock price speculation over the large revenues anticipated from them. The creation of extra votes by stock-splitting had developed on a large scale, and the whole situation was rendered more complex by the involvement of parliamentary factions in Company politics. This state of chaotic instability in the management of the Company highlighted the anomaly that a private trading company should be ruling vast territories, and made that task much more difficult. Company servants in India came to ignore the flow of contradictory orders from London, and many were able to line their own pockets. The return home as wealthy 'nabobs' of men who had gone out impecunious to India focused increasing public attention in Britain on the abuses and misrule of India under the Company.

The government interventions of 1767 and 1769 had been concerned with obtaining for the state a share in the Indian revenue.* Little had been done to reform the Company at home, although in 1769 a six-month voting qualification was imposed on stockholders. No attention had been paid at all to the problem of the government of India itself. North had brushed aside mention of this matter in 1769, and his ministry failed even to give sufficient parliamentary support to ensure the success of such minor measures as military recruiting bills sponsored by the Company in 1770 and 1771.

The North ministry's intervention in the Company was to be sparked off not by the growing public concern over mismanagement in India but by its financial weakness. The Company was faced by declining income at the same time as it incurred rising costs, notably on military expenditure as a precaution against anticipated French attacks and native troubles. The territorial revenue from Bengal had fallen sharply, and the Company's warehouses in Britain were being filled with unsold tea: yet in 1771 the Company raised its dividend to the maximum of $12\frac{1}{2}$ per cent. By the end of that year the issue of state intervention had come before the North cabinet. The Bedfordite faction led by Gower favoured this, but North was unwilling to interfere, and the ministry decided to permit the Company to mend its own affairs. The Company missed this opportunity. Its Judicature Bill, intended to remedy some administrative abuses in India, was not presented to Parliament until 30 March 1772, and by then a storm of public criticism was developing over abuses of the Company's rule in India. Faced with demands from M.P.s for an inquiry before any action was taken, North allowed the bill to lapse.

The Indian crisis broke during the parliamentary recess of 1772. The Directors had maintained their $12\frac{1}{2}$ per cent dividend in April but were obliged to suspend payment in September. The grave financial trouble, reflected in a falling stock price, led the Company to invite the government interference it had been seeking to avoid. North was at first inclined to help the Company without raising wider issues, but he soon decided that the matter would have to come before the Commons, and Parliament was summoned to meet on 26 November instead of in the following January. The Treasury meanwhile took a tough line with the Company, refusing credit and requesting information. Public opinion demanded action from the ministry, for the Company was discredited: but it was always with

* Above, pp. 18–19, 31.

reluctance that North intervened, and the opposition belief that his administration was eager to lay hands on the Indian patronage was quite unfounded. Some members of the cabinet favoured the solution of taking over the entire responsibility for the government and revenue of the territories in India. North himself always championed the principle that these belonged to the Crown and not to the Company, and considered putting it into practice at this time; but on 17 January 1773 Shelburne told Chatham that North had abandoned this idea on 'finding the friends of administration in the House of Commons very averse to it'.[48] North was well aware that such a course of action would provoke controversy at Westminster and fury at India House, and he also found a practical objection to it: the burden on governmental resources. But he was determined that any financial help for the Company would be in return for reforms in Indian administration, and the correspondence of George III and his ministers shows that their motives were not merely financial and military but also included a sense of their obligation to maintain law and order in the Indian territories of the Company. The burden of empire was being shouldered.

When Parliament met, North proposed a small secret Committee of his own supporters to prepare reports as the basis of legislation, and he gave scope to popular feeling by permitting a simultaneous open Committee under General Burgoyne to investigate past scandals. The chief obstacle to ministerial policy was not to be Parliament, since the opposition factions of Rockingham and Chatham were divided on the issue,* nor the Company's Directors, but the Court of Proprietors, where the Duke of Richmond, a leading opposition politician, sought to harass the ministry by a successful appeal to the prejudices and vested interests of stockholders. This resistance embarrassed North but did not thwart his ultimate objective. He had hoped that reform would be accepted by the Company voluntarily instead of being dictated to it by Parliament. But in February 1773 Richmond persuaded the Court of Proprietors to overrule efforts by the Directors to negotiate a settlement, and North was obliged to resort to Parliament.

The Company was asking for a loan and for customs concessions over tea exports. North was disposed to grant both requests. He proposed a loan on 9 March 1773 in the first major debate of the session on India. The state would lend the Company £1,400,000, the Treasury having arrived at this figure by deducting the anticipated commercial

---

* In brief, the Rockinghamites criticized North for interfering too much, the Chathamites for not doing enough.

profit for the year of £600,000 from the estimated current deficit of £1,900,000. North flatly stated his own opinion that any territories acquired by conquest belonged to the state, but later clarified his position by saying that the public had no claim to any trading profits. A fortnight later, on 23 March, North announced resolutions to limit the Company dividend based on those profits. It would be 6 per cent until the government loan had been repaid, and 7 per cent until the bond debt had been reduced to £1,500,000.[49] On 5 April North told the Commons of his longer term plans for the Company's revenue. While he had not changed his opinion on the right of the state to the Indian territories, he thought it the best policy for them to remain in the Company's control, under certain conditions: 'Till we find the Company cannot govern the country properly, under regulations now to be framed, I would not come to the question of right or take possession of it.' The new agreement was to run six years from the expiry of the present one in 1774 and would therefore end in 1780 when the current charter was due to expire. Moreover, the government would give up the £400,000 a year it had received from the Company since 1767. This would be 'a great loss', but 'the proper re-establishment of the Company is with me a greater object'. If the Company's profits rose above what was required for an 8 per cent dividend the state would take three quarters of any such surplus while the other quarter was to go towards debt redemption and capital accumulation.[50]

All these provisions were to be the basis of the first legislative measure, the Loan Bill. But the Company objected to the restrictions in the bill and had not proposed any administrative reorganization. North had already realized that the ministry would have to take the initiative in this respect. A draft Regulating Bill was under consideration by mid-March, and before Parliament rose for the Easter recess North moved a Call of the House summoning M.P.s to meet and be counted on 26 April. Lord of the Admiralty Thomas Bradshaw explained to a friend that North had taken this unusual step for a minister because he 'thought that the blue sky will otherwise carry all the country gentlemen home and that it will not be proper to carry important questions respecting the future regulations and management of the East India Company by a small number of placemen'.[51] This laudable objective was not to be achieved, for the squires failed to stay in town, and the East India Regulating Bill was carried in thin Houses.

On 3 May North explained the provisions of the Regulating Bill to the Commons. They concerned both the Company at home and its administration in India. North said that a principal cause of the Company's lack of authority over its servants was the annual election of Directors. He intended to alter this: henceforth six Directors would be elected each year, to serve for four years. Moreover, the stock qualification for Proprietors to vote would be doubled from £500 to £1,000, and this must be held for a year instead of six months. These reforms would prevent stock-splitting and other electoral abuses within the Company. In Bengal there was to be a Supreme Court with judges appointed by the Crown, a provision taken from the Company's own abortive Judicature Bill of 1772. The government of Bengal would be vested in a Governor-General and a Council of four members, which would also have a superintending power over the Company's other territories in India. This body would be nominated in the first instance by Parliament, with vacancies filled by the Company, subject to the veto of the ministry. The present governor of Bengal, Warren Hastings, North declared, was the obvious choice as first Governor-General.[52]

These were proposals that aroused the Company to greater fury than the financial provisions: but for the moment public attention was diverted to the question of past abuses. North himself ended his speech with a discussion of the subject that made his own attitude quite clear. 'Fortunes have been too rapidly and improperly made. No servant or free merchant should trade but for the Company.' The revelations of Burgoyne's Committee had led to a widespread feeling that proceedings should be instigated against Lord Clive as the man who had brought the greatest fortune home from India. The administration was divided on the course of action to adopt, and in debate on 10 May North said that it was not 'a proper subject to be undertaken by a First Lord of the Treasury. The minister should only judge as a Member of Parliament.'[53] North commended Burgoyne for his public spirit and wanted to see justice done, but he was at the same time anxious not to offend Clive. He therefore did not speak in the heated debates of 19 and 21 May on the motion condemning Clive, save on a procedural point:[54] but he voted in the minority in favour of the motion, which was defeated by 155 to 95. Thomas Bradshaw commented afterwards that 'it was no ministerial question. Lord North did not call for the support of any one friend. He was opposed by his warmest partisans and supported by many of his keenest enemies.'[55] North had satisfied his personal conscience, but must have felt political relief that the matter had ended.

The administration had meanwhile come to realize the need to break the deadlock with the Company, for on 14 May the Court of

Proprietors rejected the loan terms. North therefore wielded the big stick. In the Commons on 25 May he proposed resolutions that any Company profits must first be used to pay off debts, and he explained that the Company would not be allowed to pay any dividends at all unless the government loan was accepted.[56] In debate on the Loan Bill itself on 15 June, North pointed out that the creditors of the Company could have resorted to legal process, but that would have spelt ruin. He said that his aim was simply to restore the Company's credit and safety, and he was clearly anxious to correct the impression that he was an enemy of the Company: 'I am not for violent measures . . . The Company I think keep all their rights. Is it ambition to oblige any one to be saved ? . . . Parliament like an honest surgeon should do his patient good and probe to the bottom notwithstanding the cries of his patient.'[57] Later North sugared the pill by withdrawing the claim of the state to share in the Company's revenue after the reduction of the debt. This concession, and the passage of a Tea Act giving the Company permission to export tea duty-free to America,* enabled the ministry to win the eventual acquiescence of the Company in the administration's measures. North was therefore able to avoid the overt coercion of the Company that would have made difficult its future relationship with the government.

The Regulating Bill had already been passed. In the final Commons debate on 10 June, North admitted that he did not expect it to solve all the Company's problems, and he expressed the hope that the Company would now manage Indian affairs so competently that the government would not have to take over control.[58] But the intervention of the North ministry did not stop short at the legislation of 1773. Henceforth the administration, believing that India was too important to be left to the Company, engaged in political management at India House, primarily through the efforts of Lord Sandwich and Treasury Secretary John Robinson. It was all very well for North to say in debate that Parliament had often altered charters before. In 1773 the ministry had not merely taken measures to set the Company on its feet again. It had initiated a policy of continuous interference in the wealthiest and most influential commercial concern in Britain. Company politician Laurence Sulivan described North as 'the boldest minister this realm has been blest with since the days of Oliver Cromwell'.[59] This was to anticipate the long-term implications of North's policy rather than his immediate intention. In 1773 his aim was to put the Company on trial, and to

* See below, pp. 73–4.

review the situation when the charter came up for renewal in 1780. But by then his hands would be so full with other problems that India was to receive little attention.

These early years show North to best advantage as Prime Minister. Convincing in Parliament, he was also positive in government. Problems may have been tackled in a spirit of reluctant necessity, but such an attitude was characteristic of most politicians of the century and many since. Much of the credit for producing prompt and practical solutions must go to North personally, and later complaints about his indecisiveness should not be read back into this period of his ministry. How much North was involved in the details of policy remains unclear in the absence of adequate surviving correspondence. It would seem that he had already begun to rely on a group of confidential advisers, who included Charles Jenkinson, holder of a succession of second-rank offices; Treasury Secretaries John Robinson and Grey Cooper; and Jenkinson's brother-in-law Charles Cornwall, who deserted the opposition in 1773 and became a Treasury Lord the next year. Certainly Robinson and Jenkinson were engaged in much of the detailed preparation and negotiation over the Indian question, already taking much of the burden from North's shoulders in a way that was to become familiar in the closing years of the ministry. But it was North who had the final voice in what was accepted and rejected, and North who presented and explained the policy decisions as his own to the Commons. His reputation would stand high if his ministry had ended around 1774: but his responsibility for the American Revolution remains the nub of the historical condemnation of him, and the colonial crisis was not solved during these years of success.

4

THE AMERICAN CRISIS
1770-76

North's early success and solid achievements
as Prime Minister have been overshadowed by the responsibility of
his administration for the American Revolution. When everything
else has been said, he remains in historical memory as 'the minister
who lost America'. The charge against him falls into two parts:
failure to prevent the colonial revolt and failure to subdue the
rebellion once it had occurred. Recently there have been attempts to
exonerate him, and not without success on the second count. It is
now realized that North had little personal concern in the conduct of
the American War, even though, like Sir Robert Walpole in a
similar situation forty years earlier, he had to pay the political price

as head of the ministry for its failure.* North's responsibility for the coming of the American Revolution is another matter. He was closely involved in policy decisions at every stage of the escalating crisis. Mitigating circumstances have been emphasized by modern scholars: the inevitability of the demand of settlement colonies for independence, and the restriction on his freedom of action imposed by the near-unanimity of contemporary public opinion in Britain on the issue of the subordination of the colonies to the mother country. But even when allowance is made for such considerations there remain the questions of how far North himself was responsible for the problem and of whether he had any practical ideas or even intention of solving it other than by force.

The policy North inherited as minister was the one he had helped to shape in the fateful Grafton cabinet meeting of 1 May 1769, the decision to retain the tea duty but to repeal the other Townshend duties and at the same time to announce to the colonies that there would be no new taxation for revenue in the future. This was not the decision to abandon an American revenue altogether that has commonly been assumed by historians. In North's mind the tea duty was retained not merely as a symbol of Parliament's right of taxation but also to provide the financial resources for implementing Charles Townshend's plan for the payment of British salaries to colonial governors, judges and other officials. His ministry was to carry out the proposal fully in Massachusetts and to some extent in other colonies.

Not until the political crisis of early 1770 was over did North seek parliamentary approval for the alteration of the Townshend duties. A circular letter sent by Hillsborough to the colonies on 13 May 1769 had already made this intention public knowledge, and the administration faced some criticism among its own supporters. There was resentment at what seemed a presumptuous pledge of parliamentary opinion, and a widespread belief that the policy was too lenient towards the colonies. North knew also that the policy would be attacked by opposition members on the ground that anything less than total repeal of the tax would not end colonial resistance. Simultaneous criticism of North's American policy for being too hard and too soft was to be his fate in the years ahead.

North introduced the subject to the Commons in 5 March 1770. He began by denouncing the American trade boycotts as 'illegal combinations', but went on to argue that everyone would wish to remove duties harmful to the British economy. It was a recurrent

* North's role in the war is discussed in the next chapter.

theme of his speech that anger at American behaviour should not mislead Parliament into retaining a tax upon Britain's own manufactures like glass and paint. North explained that Hillsborough's circular had been intended to allay colonial fears, and regretted that it had not produced peace and obedience in America. Acts of violence and illegal combinations had continued, and any further concessions were out of the question: 'The Americans, by their subsequent behaviour, have not deserved any particular indulgence from this country.' North voiced the opinion that if the Stamp Act had not been repealed it would then be in effective operation, and announced: 'I never will be driven to repeal a duty by downright force.' North then put the positive case for retaining the tea duty. Tea was not a British product: it was a luxury: and the 3d. duty was light. Moreover, the tea duty was producing over £11,000 a year and would 'go a great way towards effecting the purpose for which it was laid; which was to give additional support to our government and judicatures in America'. North was avowedly adopting Townshend's aim of depriving the colonial assemblies of their financial weapon against the executive.

Loss of trade was the main reason urged for complete repeal, North said, and he put forward political and economic arguments to counter it. The Americans wanted repeal in order to establish their claim that Britain had no right to raise a revenue from them: 'This being the case, I cannot consent to give up the point.' Even total repeal would not satisfy the colonists: they would next complain of the Revenue Acts of 1764 and 1766 imposing the molasses duty, and the same point of dispute over taxation would still remain after a disgraceful surrender. In any case, he claimed, the recent fall in exports to America was deceptive, because the colonists had been stocking up beforehand. Already some American prices had risen sharply, and some boycotts had been relaxed or broken. Rather than give way to such pressure he would counter-attack by stronger measures against smuggling and by legislation to prevent colonial manufactures. Then came his peroration: 'I wish to be thought what I really am, to the best of my conviction – a friend to trade, a friend to America.'

The ensuing debate was confused. Thomas Pownall moved an amendment to add repeal of the tea duty. Grenville announced that he could support neither North's motion nor the amendment, and blamed the administration for having no American plan: he was to lead his friends out of the House before the vote. North denied the imputation of appeasement, weakly saying that no one had proposed a plan. Grenville tartly rejoined that that was the duty of the minister. Retention of the tea duty was attacked by Conway, who led a group of five administration supporters to vote for its repeal. More significant discontent on the government side was voiced by office-holders like Welbore Ellis, who opposed any repeal, and Lord Barrington, who argued that repeal should be confined to those colonies that had obeyed the law. Opposition speakers Rockingham-ite Sir William Meredith and Chathamite Barré both spoke for complete repeal. The House divided over Pownall's amendment, and the ministry won by a majority of only sixty-two votes, 204 to 142.[1]

North maintained a low profile of evasion and concession when opposition members pressed the American question in Parliament later that session. He refused to debate again the repeal of the tea duty when London merchant M.P. Barlow Trecothick proposed it on 9 April; accepted with modifications a motion by Trecothick on 26 April for papers about the 'Boston Massacre' of 5 March;* and agreed to a motion made by Edmund Burke on 1 May for papers on colonial reactions to Hillsborough's circular of the previous year.[2] His attempt to take the heat out of the American question was successful, for the ministry defeated with ease the only major opposition attack, when on 9 May Burke proposed a series of eight resolutions condemning such recent measures as the dissolution of colonial assemblies. Burke declared that he had postponed his action in the vain hope of some initiative from the ministry, and the main theme of opposition speakers was the administration's lack of an American policy. Grenvillite Henry Seymour accused North of treating the colonial question as 'a trifle'. North had apparently dropped off to sleep by the time Edmund Burke's kinsman William Burke spoke, for he made this comment: 'I wish the noble lord opposite had some one at his elbow, to pull him every now and then by the ear, and give him a gentle tap on the shoulder . . . to keep him awake to the affairs of America.' When North rose to make the administration reply he claimed that the partial repeal of the Townshend duties had been 'the best measure that could be carried this session', an implicit promise of further action that raised unfounded hopes on all sides. North made the most of the fact that some of his critics favoured a harder line towards the colonies and others more leniency: what other plan should he adopt, he asked ironically? Grenville then rose for what was to prove his last parliamentary speech, a scathing

---

* On that day exasperated British soldiers had fired on a taunting mob and killed five civilians, an incident that led to the enforced withdrawal of troops from the town.

attack on North's attitude: 'I have seen many administrations, but the present are the only ministers who uniformly substitute personalities in the place of argument. Oppose their measures, and their constant answer is "Oh! You want to be minister."' Nothing could be worse than the inactivity of the present ministry, Grenville said, prophetically warning North that 'to his neglect the King may owe the loss of America'.[3] This opposition onslaught had no effect on parliamentary opinion or ministerial policy. North won the only division of the day by 199 votes to 79: and in the longer term the policy adopted by the North administration seemed to have been a shrewd calculation. The American trade boycotts collapsed by the end of 1770, and little was heard of trouble in the colonies for some years. Not until 1773 did Parliament again debate America.

This superficial improvement in the imperial relationship after 1770 concealed a simmering discontent in the colonies. There was continuous resentment at the enforcement of the trade laws, highlighted from time to time by violent incidents, the most notorious of them the burning of the revenue schooner *Gaspée* in June 1772 after it had run aground chasing smugglers at Rhode Island. The North ministry could not overlook such an outrage, and established a Commission of Inquiry: this discovered nothing, and led to the evolution of an inter-colonial network of Committees of Correspondence. More ominous was the revival of a direct constitutional clash as a result of the policy of the North administration. Colonial opinion had never lost sight of the conflict that had surfaced in the earlier quarrels over taxation. The colonists had come to regard their assemblies as mini-Parliaments, with rights of taxation and legislation comparable to those of the Parliament at Westminster. British public opinion could not accept any interpretation of the structure of empire other than that Parliament had sovereign power over all parts of the King's dominions. This was the basic cause of the American Revolution, and it was brought to the fore once again by the decision of the North ministry to implement as far as funds would allow Charles Townshend's plan for the payment of colonial officials from the revenue duties he had imposed in 1767. A start had already been made in 1768, with the payment of Exchequer salaries to the Attorney-General of New York and the Chief Justice of Massachusetts. In 1770 this practice was extended to the Governors of New York and Massachusetts and in 1772 to the Chief Justices of New York and New Jersey. 1772 also saw the use of the fund, now drawn solely from the tea duty, to pay the salaries of the Attorney-General, Solicitor-General and five lower judges in Massachusetts.[4]

This deliberate attempt to control the civil list of that colony was a threat to the financial hold of the provincial legislature over the royal executive and judiciary. It led to a petition from the Massachusetts Assembly to the Crown, and although the new Colonial Secretary Dartmouth persuaded Massachusetts agent Benjamin Franklin to withdraw the petition temporarily, there followed a public debate in early 1773 between Governor Thomas Hutchinson and the Massachusetts Council and Assembly about the authority of Parliament. Hutchinson unwisely opened the discussion by a speech seeking to demonstrate that the colonies, as part of the British dominions, were subject to Parliament: 'I know of no line that can be drawn between the supreme authority of Parliament and the total independence of the colonies.' This assertion provoked replies from the Council and the Assembly which asserted that the colony's charter limited the power of Parliament. The British cabinet was alarmed at this open challenge to parliamentary supremacy, and during the spring of 1773 thought of submitting the relevant papers to the Commons. The intention, North told Hutchinson the following year, would have been to change the constitution of the colony in much the same way as was to be done in the Massachusetts Government Act of 1774.[5] The reform deemed most necessary concerned the Council. Massachusetts was the only colony where a royal governor was confronted by a Council elected by the Assembly and not assisted by one nominated by the Crown; and a move to change this state of affairs had long been advocated by politicians and officials with knowledge of America. The administration finally decided to do nothing, because attendance at debates was already dwindling and the attention of those M.P.s remaining was engrossed by the affairs of the East India Company: but that the ministry was contemplating any such action at this time is a significant indication of the hardening of the government attitude on America even before the spectacular act of colonial defiance involved in the Boston Tea Party. When Franklin presented both the original and a second Massachusetts petition on the salaries grievance to Dartmouth in May 1773 he met with a complete rebuff: and the next month Dartmouth told Hutchinson that the Treasury would cease payment of the salaries only if the Assembly made a permanent settlement of adequate salaries on the Governor and judges to replace the annual provision of them. The ministerial intention to deprive the Assembly of its financial weapon was manifestly clear.

Already North had refused to bow to parliamentary pressure for cancellation of the tea tax which provided the money for the colonial salaries. At the end of 1772 the East India Company had built up a stock of about 18,000,000 lb. of tea, nearly three years' domestic supply. By January 1773 the Company planned to ask the administration for a cancellation of the export duty, intending to dump surplus tea cheaply in Europe: but a month later the realization that this might be smuggled back to Britain and kill the home market led the Company to think of America, where most of the tea being consumed was smuggled from Holland. A petition from the Company to Parliament on 2 March asked for permission to export tea there free of any British duty although not of the 3d. Townshend duty. This proposal would remove duties amounting to about 9d. a lb. and enable the Company's tea to undersell the Dutch tea, or so it was believed.

The ministry accepted the scheme, and North presented it to the House of Commons on 26 April. He found himself assailed by a barrage of criticism over the retention of the Townshend duty. Dowdeswell, Trecothick and others argued that the opportunity to sell 2,000,000 lb of tea a year to America would be jeopardized and the whole aim of bringing financial relief to the East India Company frustrated. North, aware that some 300,000 lb of dutied tea a year was being sold in America, denied that the Townshend duty had any significant effect on the market there and announced that he was not willing to give up this method of financing the costs of civil government in America. He anticipated that the change would produce a large increase in the revenue from this duty, and refused to consider its repeal until he was convinced that there was no possibility of having an American revenue. That North also valued the tea duty as a token of British sovereignty was shown by his reply to a suggestion from Dowdeswell that if revenue was his aim a better method would be to retain 3d. a lb from the British export duty. He said that there were 'political reasons' for retaining the Townshend duty in its present form, adding that 'the temper of the people there is little deserving favour from hence'.[6]

The hardening attitude of the British government on the American question was therefore apparent before further colonial defiance later in 1773. Official opinion was then exasperated by the affair of 'the Hutchinson letters'. Some private correspondence to Britain written by Governor Hutchinson, his deputy Andrew Oliver and others during the later 1760s had come into the hands of Benjamin Franklin: the letters contained frankly hostile comments on events in Massachusetts by the men now in high office there. Franklin had sent them to Boston, where they were read out in the Massachusetts Assembly, which then sent a petition to the King for the dismissal of Hutchinson and Oliver. The Privy Council postponed the matter until after the Christmas recess; and before it heard the case on 29 January 1774 news had arrived of the Boston Tea Party.

Although taxed tea had hitherto been bought in Massachusetts more commonly than elsewhere, what was regarded in America as the attempt of the British government to force the issue of taxation had provoked violence there. On the night of 16 December a mob boarded the three tea ships in Boston harbour and threw the tea into the water. The action symbolized universal colonial hostility, and similar action did not occur elsewhere only because it was unnecessary: at other ports ships did not arrive or left in haste. But to British opinion it seemed that once again Boston was the leader of resistance. News of the incident had come by 19 January and at once gave rise to widespread demands for coercion. The cabinet was united on this point: if Suffolk, Gower and Sandwich expressed themselves most forcibly, North and Dartmouth were as determined as their colleagues to assert the sovereignty of Parliament over America. North later told Hutchinson that he had abandoned his customary practice of sounding colonial opinion before taking action because the facts were 'so gross and so notorious'.[7] The Privy Council meeting of 29 January on the Massachusetts petition took place in a heated atmosphere and was highlighted by an abusive attack on Franklin by Solicitor-General Wedderburn that received an enthusiastic reception: only North, it would seem, behaved with 'decent gravity': and the rejection of the petition was a foregone conclusion.

It was Dartmouth, as the minister responsible for the colonies, who in cabinet on 4 February made the first two proposals concerning Boston, the removal of the Massachusetts Assembly from the malign atmosphere of that town and the closure of its harbour by the transfer of the customs office elsewhere. Dartmouth assumed that both could be achieved by executive action. He also hoped to punish those responsible for the riot by due process of law, and the cabinet instructed the Attorney- and Solicitor-Generals to consider the evidence. These ideas combined promptness with moderation, a course of action that avoided the delay and provocation of fresh legislation: but this remedy proved to be impracticable. The law officers reported that there was insufficient evidence for the trial of any persons, and the cabinet on 28 February accepted this opinion with reluctance. North afterwards expressed public regret, in the House of Commons, that the direct punishment of individuals had not been possible. Already the cabinet had had second thoughts on the method of closing Boston harbour. Doubts about the legality of using the royal prerogative had led to a decision on 19 February for an Act of Parliament. This was an abandonment of a more moderate policy in favour of a clear demonstration of Parliament's right to legislate for the colonies. The cabinet also decided upon a bill to alter the Massachusetts constitution. The behaviour of the colony's Council in once again refusing to support the Governor now silenced any objection: North and Dartmouth agreed with their colleagues on the need to convert the Council into a body nominated by the Crown. During early March other provisions were added to what became the Massachusetts Government Bill, clauses to end the system of elected juries, to prevent town meetings without the Governor's consent, and to give the Governor nomination of the colony's law officers; for North was persuaded by former Massachusetts Governor Sir Francis Bernard that these changes were also necessary to establish a balance in the colony between the executive and the legislature.[8]

The Boston Port Bill was meanwhile drafted by North and Dartmouth, and introduced by North in the Commons on 14 March. It was a temporary measure, he said, and would continue only until compensation had been paid to the East India Company. He cited such precedents for punishment of whole communities for similar offences as the fine on Edinburgh for the Porteous Riots of 1737. Here is diarist Brickdale's summary of North's case against Boston:

It has been the ringleader of all violence and opposition to the execution of the laws of this country. New York and Philadelphia grew unruly on receiving the news of the triumph of the people of Boston. Boston has not only therefore to answer for its own violence but for having incited other places to tumults.

North argued that the dispute between Britain and her colonies was no longer about taxation: 'They deny our legislative authority. Not all the places but there are those who hold and defend that doctrine. If they deny authority in one instance it goes to all. We must control them or submit to them.' The debate assured North that the House was behind his policy. Most critics of the bill deemed it too moderate, while spokesmen of both opposition factions voiced support. Chathamite Barré gave the bill a warm welcome, and most Rockinghamite speakers expressed guarded approval, although Dowdeswell thought the measure unwise.[9]

The bill secured a speedy passage through Parliament and became law before Easter without a vote being cast against it. The only debate of substance took place in Committee on 23 March, when

Rose Fuller suggested the alternative punishment of a fine. North defended his mode of action as practical, for it could be enforced by 'four or five frigates'; but frankly admitted that he could not guarantee success: 'I cannot answer whether submission or rebellion will be the consequence.'[10] North had got off to a good start, as Edmund Burke told New York on 6 April: 'Lord North has assumed a style of authority, and more decision, and the Bill laying Boston under a commercial interdict during the King's pleasure has been proposed, and supported quite through, with expressions of the utmost firmness and resolution.'[11]

North introduced the Massachusetts Government Bill in the Commons on 15 April, and on the same day announced a third measure, the Massachusetts Justice Bill, explaining that the intention was to give every soldier and official in the colony prosecuted for carrying out their duties 'a fair and impartial trial': if necessary, it could be transferred to another colony or even back to Britain. This measure had been requested by the army Commander-in-Chief, General Thomas Gage, who was also to be the new Governor of Massachusetts. The new legislation met with greater parliamentary resistance than the Boston Port Act: but the opposition factions reserved their main attack for the third reading of the Government Bill on 2 May. The highlight of a ten-hour debate was the opening speech by Dunning, who argued that the constitutional changes proposed would not solve the problem of colonial discontent, and that the two bills were respectively provocative and repressive. North spoke near the end, skilfully exaggerating the wider and wilder opposition arguments to the point of absurdity. He poured scorn on the apparent assumption of some M.P.s that Boston had a right to plunder British ships: asserted that it was impossible to expect fair trials in the colony at the time; denied that he was seeking to establish a military government; and expressed amazement that the subject of colonial taxation should have been debated at all. His administration secured a massive vote of confidence in its American policy, by a majority of 239 to 64.[12] A challenge to the Massachusetts Justice Bill four days later was brushed aside by 127 votes to 24, Rose Fuller admitting in despair that not only Parliament but public opinion was behind the administration policy: 'It is not an error of the ministry, it is an error of the nation. I see it wherever I go.'[13] North himself later told Hutchinson that he had taken the opportunity to pass the legislation 'when all persons of all parties were of the same mind' and that much of the parliamentary battle had been sham: 'That, in general, whatever measure had been proposed by the ministers, had also been opposed: but that all parties united in the necessity of a change, in order to prevent the colony from entirely throwing off their dependence.'[14]

The Quebec Act was passed immediately after the Massachusetts legislation, and was widely regarded in Britain and America as another coercive measure: but the North ministry had already intended to pass the bill that session. Plans for the government of the colony, taken from France in the Seven Years' War, had been in gestation for a decade, and many of the enlightened provisions concerning the French Catholic population had been formulated by the Rockingham administration in 1766. The North ministry asked its law officers for a Quebec plan in 1771, and had their reports under consideration during much of 1773. By August of that year North had decided to implement the proposals during the next parliamentary session. The measure was generous and far-sighted, avoiding the creation of another Irish situation. It permitted the French majority the free exercise of their Roman Catholic religion, including the levying of tithes, and the retention of their old civil laws. But they were denied full political rights. North in 1773 insisted that the form of government should be a nominated Council, because any Assembly would have been composed of Catholics: but the decision exposed his ministry to the charge of establishing in North America a form of government that was not merely Popish but despotic. Worse still for its impact on colonial opinion was the extension of the boundary southward to the Ohio river. Intended to protect the Indian lands from settler encroachments, this change sealed off the older northern colonies from further expansion. The decision to implement all these provisions by legislation had been taken before news of the Boston Tea Party. The Quebec Bill then had to be postponed because of the American crisis: but the ministry knew the importance of conciliating the French Canadians at a time of conflict with the older British colonies, and introduced the measure late in the session.

The Quebec Bill passed first through the House of Lords, and was not debated in the Commons until its second reading on 26 May. North explained that the bill had already been long delayed by the need for full information. No one could deny that the colony needed a system of government, and it was better to restore the old Ohio boundary than to create a new colony south of the Great Lakes. North then defended the other two clauses that incurred particular criticism: all British colonies were allowed the free exercise of their religion, but any elected Assembly would necessarily have been

Papist.[15] Already the ministry had taken care to meet one obvious objection on this last point by denying the nominated Council the right of taxation, and the next day North proposed Canadian import duties for the financial support of the civil government in the colony.[16] North was also prepared to be conciliatory about the boundary grievances of the older colonies. On 31 May he agreed to hear the complaints of Pennsylvania and New York. In Committee on 6 June he himself proposed a general amendment to prevent encroachment on the older colonies by establishing a commission to settle disputes on the spot. This was too vague to satisfy critics like Edmund Burke, speaking in his role as New York agent. North argued that Parliament would not be able to fix exact boundaries, but later conceded the point and at the report stage on 10 June allowed Burke to push through a detailed boundary clause.[17] These arguments and concessions failed to avert a torrent of criticism from a small but vociferous band of opponents. It took nine days of debate before North got the bill through the Commons by 13 June, even though the highest opposition vote was a mere forty-nine. He himself undertook the defence of the measure almost single-handed, making seventy-two speeches during its passage. North deserves great credit for this public defiance of popular prejudice even though he had no personal responsibility for the more enlightened provisions of the bill. He showed political sagacity in his timing, which assured the passive loyalty of the French Canadians during the American Revolution. But the measure had its part in increasing colonial discontent; and the clauses which the North ministry introduced, concerning the Council and the boundary, were among those that gave most offence to the older colonies.

The legislation of 1774 led to the final escalation of the American crisis. The parliamentary opposition had agreed on the need for some such demonstration of British authority as the Boston Port Act, but had then criticized the Massachusetts legislation, arguing that there ought to be some conciliatory move, notably the repeal of the tea duty. The option was not open to North, for the state of British political opinion made any such policy unacceptable to Parliament. When Thomas Hutchinson, who had just resigned as Governor of Massachusetts, arrived in Britain on 30 June, he immediately became aware of the intransigent mood he encountered almost everywhere he went, and he thought it would be impossible to reconcile this feeling with the state of colonial opinion he had just left behind. The ministers themselves were certainly aware that their policy was a gamble, based on the hope rather than the expectation that Massachusetts would not resist and that, if she did, the other colonies would not rally round her. They were resolved to face a confrontation if one arose: even the moderate Dartmouth thought that an example should be made of such leaders as John Hancock and Sam Adams when news came of the first colonial reactions to the American measures.[18]

North himself was neither a mere prisoner of events nor a moderate spurred on by bellicose colleagues. That he was determined on resolute action is known to us from the diary of Thomas Hutchinson, who discussed America with the Prime Minister on several occasions during the summer of 1774. On 7 July Hutchinson found North adamant that the colonies needed correction and regretful only that such chastisement had been so long delayed; and on 3 August he sent this comment back to his son: 'Lord North gives himself no concern, or at least he appears unconcerned, and says that order and government must take place in the colonies, whether it be sooner or later depends upon themselves: in the meantime they can hurt nobody but themselves.' North's opinion that the colonies were unable to strike at Britain proved a sound assessment: their trade boycott failed to generate any significant reaction in Britain, whose merchants and manufacturers were discovering alternative markets in Europe and farther afield. News of the early colonial resistance to British policy did not cause North to change his attitude. He commented to Hutchinson that he did not consider the 1774 legislation 'less necessary than he did before', and said that 'he was not apprehensive' of the Congress summoned to meet at Philadelphia in September. On 21 September North told Hutchinson that the Boston rioters must be punished and that some way should be found to punish also those concerned in the Congress. If the Congress decided on a non-importation agreement, he said, then 'Great Britain would take care they should trade nowhere else. And if any colonies stood out, all encouragement should be given such colonies.'[19] North already had in mind what was to be his administration's riposte to the trade boycott that was to be established by the Congress.

Before any policy was implemented the ministry decided upon a general election: for one was due in or before March 1775 and would then interrupt the normal pattern of parliamentary business. A dissolution had been contemplated as early as May, when North opposed the idea. He still did not favour the proposal when it was under consideration from the second half of August, and his doubts were not allayed by consultations with John Robinson, the Secretary to the Treasury who had immediate responsibility for electoral and

parliamentary management. On 27 September North warned
George III that although 'many good consequences will result from
a sudden dissolution' the lack of preparation would mean the loss of
some seats.[20] But two days later he acquiesced in a cabinet decision
for an immediate election, and this was announced on 30 September.
North himself was influenced by the American situation, for he
afterwards told Hutchinson that the motive had been 'that we
might, at the beginning of a Parliament, take such measures as we
could depend upon a Parliament to prosecute to effect'.[21]

North shared with Robinson the management of the government
election campaign, and had to do a great deal of the detailed work
himself when Robinson fell ill. The election was not fought on a
national basis or on the American issue, which was mentioned in
only a few constituencies. In the eighteenth century seats were
contested or controlled at local level, and participation by the ministry was limited to a small proportion of the constituencies, and
to three chief modes of action. The administration had to arrange
suitable candidates for the score of seats in 'government boroughs':
even these were not altogether safe, and North had to compromise at
Dover in 1774 by conceding one of the two seats in order to retain
the other. Secondly, the ministry negotiated with private patrons
who supplied seats for official nominees in return for money or
favours: and, thirdly, it sought to win large constituencies in order
to be able to claim popular support. This last aspect of the ministerial
campaign in 1774 was a failure: no candidate could be found for
Middlesex, and those backed in London and Bristol were defeated.
In one way or another North distributed some £50,000 to help
various supporters with their expenses, but this sum was a small
proportion of the total amount of money spent at a general election.
The 'government interest' could not be more than a makeweight in
the balance of electoral forces. This did not matter in 1774. When the
results were known by mid-November, North's conservative estimate
to the King was that administration had 321 safe supporters out of
the House of 558 M.P.s.[22]

Before the election was over the magnitude of the American
problem had become apparent. In October Gage reported that the
Massachusetts Government Act was being rendered unworkable by
evasion and obstruction: warned that the opposition came not from
a mob but from men of property: and asked for more soldiers.
North admitted the case for reinforcements but told Gage that it
would take a year to provide them; and in a moment of prescience
doubted the wisdom of a military land strategy to control North

America. Dartmouth favoured sending more ships, and these reached Boston in December. Government opinion hardened during the next few weeks. News came on 10 November of the non-importation agreement decided on by the Congress, and North told Hutchinson that 'now the case seemed desperate. Parliament would not, could not, concede. For aught he could see it must come to violence.' North's anger increased when Gage advised the temporary suspension of the 1774 Acts, which he insisted 'must and should be carried into execution'. He commented to Hutchinson on 19 November that 'it was to no purpose any longer to think of expedients: the province was in actual rebellion, and must be subdued. He would not allow the thought that the kingdom was not able to do it.' When Boston radical Josiah Quincy visited North on his arrival in London that month the Prime Minister told him that he and the rest of the cabinet were determined to enforce Parliament's authority: 'If he should yield the point, he should expect to have his head brought to the block by the general clamour of the people and he should deserve it. This must be submitted to, and then he would give the most favourable ear to every proposal from the colonies.'[23] The ministry was already doubtful whether Gage was the right man for the task; but in November the cabinet negatived a proposal by Suffolk for his recall, North preferring to send capable subordinates to put some backbone into the Commander-in-Chief. By the end of the year North had become convinced of the need to replace Gage, and it was only the difficulty of finding a successor that left him in his post for so long.

Until December of 1774 North shared with his colleagues and sovereign a conviction in the need for firm measures to enforce British sovereignty before consideration would be given to colonial grievances. But that month saw a significant change in his attitude to the American question. Realization that Britain was on the verge of civil war with her colonies caused North to draw back from the brink and embark on a new line of policy: and after the American War had begun, North portrayed himself as a moderate who had offered conciliation before the outbreak of fighting. Hutchinson at this time certainly became aware that North was seeking some way to avoid a direct confrontation. He heard a rumour that North was 'more backward than most of the rest of the ministers', and North's brother-in-law Whitshed Keene even talked of giving up the colonies to avoid the expense of subduing them. North himself commented hopefully to Hutchinson on 22 December that the Petition to the King from Congress 'did not deny the right'. Hutchinson pointed out that other documents issued by the Congress did so, and afterwards made this note on the conversation:[24]

> I could plainly perceive that it would have been very agreeable to him to have found something in the Petition that would lead to an accommodation: and if it had not been for the extravagance of the Resolves, Association and Address, passed by this Convention, notwithstanding the illegality of their assembling, which would have been winked at, the Petition would have been attended to.

Dartmouth also favoured some peaceful settlement with America, and it was doubtless after consultation with his step-brother that North had already suggested to George III a step that combined a conciliatory gesture with only mild pressure: his idea was to suspend bounties and other economic regulations favourable to the colonies, and then to send a Commission to America 'to examine into the disputes'. The King replied that the Commission would look like 'the Mother Country being more afraid of the continuance of the dispute than the Colonies'.[25] No policy decisions were taken until after the Christmas holidays had given ministers time to reflect and to acquire more information: but on 13 January 1775 the cabinet did begin to devise measures. It decided to send Gage more soldiers and to prepare legislation that would prohibit the colonies from trading and fishing, and rejected the proposal, then made by Dartmouth, to dispatch a Commission to the colonies to negotiate a settlement. The next week North did persuade the cabinet to adopt a policy of conciliation. North's plan was that Britain would promise not to tax the colonies if in return they agreed to pay the cost of their own civil governments, courts of law, and defence.[26] It embodied the significant concession of the right of the assemblies to tax themselves, one that a decade earlier might well have sufficed to allay colonial discontent. It was a practical attempt to define a solution acceptable to Britain, and a real change of heart for North, who in August 1774 had assured Hutchinson of his continued determination to pay the salaries of colonial officials and to do this from the Exchequer if the tea duty revenue proved inadequate.[27]

North's assumption that taxation was still the root cause of the dispute doomed his efforts to failure: for the response of the Congress to the so-called Coercive Acts of 1774 had been to deny the right of Parliament to legislate for the colonies at all. His policy was criticized as unacceptable by colonists and their friends in Britain at the time, and was never likely to have won favour in Massachusetts, even if news of it had arrived before fighting commenced. That North's measure of conciliation failed to match colonial demands was due to his faulty analysis of the crisis and not to the twin handicaps of bellicose colleagues and of a Parliament adamant on the assertion of its rights. For the official policy of 1775 undoubtedly bore North's personal stamp. He himself had devised, or at least promptly adopted, both the coercion by blockade and the concession over taxation. It was less conciliatory than he later sought to depict. The offer was to be available to each colony individually, and therefore open to the charge of being a tactic to shatter American unity. Any announcement of the tax concession was withheld until the coercive measures had been accepted by Parliament. There is indeed reason to think that North was concerned with the political situation in Britain rather than the colonial dispute. For on 19 February, the day before he introduced the plan to the Commons, he explained his motives to George III: 'Lord North hopes for great utility (if not in America, at least on this side of the water) to arise to the public from this motion. He is confident it gives up no right, and that it contains precisely the plan which ought to be adopted by Great Britain; even if all America were subdued.' North evidently did envisage the taxation plan as the final solution to the colonial problem after the restoration of British authority: but its immediate importance was that 'it would give general satisfaction here'.[28]

In Parliament the opposition had been pressing for a debate on America before the Christmas recess, and on 5 December North promised the Commons American papers as soon as possible.[29] A judicious selection, omitting some of Gage's comments, was laid before Parliament on 19 January. Realization among M.P.s of the gravity of the colonial crisis was reflected in an attendance estimated at 430 members when North outlined his administration's proposals on 2 February. In the Commons Committee on America he moved an Address to the Crown that emphasized the misbehaviour of the colonists and declared Massachusetts to be in a state of rebellion. There was no more than a vague reference to any intention of 'indulgence', and North in his speech mentioned only the proposed measures of coercion: 'To send more force, to bring in a temporary act to put a stop to all the foreign trade of New England, particularly to their fishery on the banks of Newfoundland, till they returned to their duty.' Redress of grievances could be considered only after submission. North said that the question was simply whether Britain should abandon or enforce sovereignty. In the ensuing debate Charles Fox moved an amendment asserting that the proposed measures would widen rather than heal the dispute between Britain and America. This was rejected by 304 votes to 105 before the Committee passed North's motion by 296 to 106.[30] When the Address was reported to the House on 6 February Chathamite Barré warned M.P.s: 'You are this night to decide whether you are to make war on your colonies.' In his reply North tried to explain his policy: 'Professed good intentions, but did not seem to promise much success in his measures. He made some distinctions between his administration and the Duke of Grafton's. Said he did not mean to tax America. And added, if they would submit, and leave to us the constitutional right of supremacy, the quarrel would be at an end.'[31] Here was the first public hint of conciliation, and of the abandonment of the attempt at colonial taxation.

North introduced the New England Trade and Fisheries Bill on 1 February, 'declaring that as the Americans had refused to trade with this kingdom it was but just that we should not suffer them to trade with any other nation'. He warned M.P.s that there was evidence of intended armed resistance in all the four New England colonies to which the bill applied, and emphasized that the measure was intended to be temporary, until the end of the year or of the next session of Parliament. The House approved the bill by 261 votes to 85.[32] The ministry next formulated its conciliation proposals, adding to the renunciation of parliamentary taxation the offer of a pardon to all colonists guilty of rebellion who submitted within a month and promised obedience to parliamentary legislation; but the requirement of such an explicit declaration robbed the offer of all practical significance. North introduced his conciliation plan in the Commons on 20 February, taking the unusual step of informing the opposition leaders of the measure beforehand and asking them to attend the debate.[33] His attempt at consensus politics rebounded on his head. Government supporters were annoyed by his failure to prepare them for the plan, opposition M.P.s encouraged by his apparent timidity.

North depicted his motion as part of an integrated policy and not a belated afterthought. He would not negotiate or compromise on the question of Britain's authority over the colonies, but believed that the taxation issue might be resolved in this way: for the resolution 'marked the ground on which negotiations could take place'. Much of North's speech was directed towards his own side of the House rather than to the opposition. He emphasized that he was proposing merely a suspension of the exercise of the right of taxation; denied that all colonists were rebels; and gave a reassurance that the policies already approved would be enforced. A number of his supporters nevertheless attacked North's motion as the first step towards the abandonment of British sovereignty, North was forced to rise several times to answer this criticism, and afterwards pointed out to the King that this behaviour was 'a strong proof that the disposition of the House independent of any ministerial connection is to maintain the authority of Great Britain over America'. North had the support of these hardliners against the opposition under Fox, who denounced the proposal as deceptive, and triumphed in the division by 274 votes to 88.[34] But his concern over the feeling on his own back benches was reflected in his speech on the report of the resolutions on 27 February. He then explicitly said that if the colonies failed to respond to the offer he would continue the tea tax and the coercive legislation.[35] When news came that other colonies had adopted the New England trade boycott the ministry decided to extend the prohibition to them. This second Restraining Bill was introduced by North on 9 March and named five more colonies. Those colonies excluded, notably New York, were so treated because bad news had not come from them and the administration hoped for a break in the colonial ranks.

In 1775 North said little on the counter-proposals put forward by opposition spokesmen. He could not, of course, reply to Chatham in the Lords, and he did not speak in the debate of 22 March on the conciliation plan put forward by Edmund Burke on behalf of the Rockingham party and defeated by 270 votes to 78. Despite Burke's fine and famous oratory, 'great empires and little minds go ill together', this proposal was also based, as was that of Chatham, on the assumption that the dispute was about taxation and no more an answer to the American problem than North's own policy. North did rise on 27 March, however, to speak against a motion by David Hartley calling for suspension of the 1774 legislation and a return to the old inefficient system of the royal 'requisition' of money from individual colonies. This practice North denounced as comparable to the notorious Ship-Money levied by Charles I, and the motion was negatived without a vote.[36]

North may have devised the policy of 1775, but the limit to his freedom of action was made clear when there arrived on 4 May from the New York Assembly a Petition to the King, Memorial to the Lords, and Remonstrance to the Commons. Here was the dutiful application that North had been hoping for, and from a colony that had rejected the decision of Congress. The Remonstrance, it is true, contained a long list of complaints about British policy since 1763, and claimed 'an exemption from internal taxation, and the exclusive right of providing for the support of our own civil government, and the administration of justice in this colony'. But it did express a willingness to pay what was required, and looked to Parliament for a redress of grievances. Dartmouth was in favour of considering the request, and Hillsborough thought North 'inclined' to do the same: but any hopes North had of building a basis of reconciliation on this slender foundation of the New York petitions were frustrated by his own supporters. On 10 May 'a meeting of the principal members of the House of Commons' decided to reject the Remonstrance because it explicitly denied Parliament's right of taxation.[37] When Edmund Burke submitted the Remonstrance to the Commons on 15 May North himself put forward this formal argument with evident reluctance. Here is a contemporary summary of his speech:

Lord North spoke greatly in favour of New York, and said that he would gladly do everything in his power to show his regard to the good behaviour of that colony: but the honour of Parliament required, that no paper should be presented to that House, which tended to call in question the unlimited rights of Parliament.

The Remonstrance was then rejected by 186 votes to 67.[38]

The significant part of the British government's American policy in 1775 was not North's conciliatory proposal but the ministerial determination to enforce colonial subordination by military repression. The cabinet was prepared to risk war, and fighting began before news of North's taxation offer reached America. A letter sent by Dartmouth on 27 January urging Gage to prevent further disorder arrived in Boston on 16 April. Three days later the first shots were fired at Lexington when a British force was on the road from Boston to destroy an arms store at Concord, and thereafter a state of war existed, with the British army besieged in Boston. News of the skirmish reached Britain on 27 May, the day after Parliament had risen for the summer recess. North took little notice of it, expressing the hope to Dartmouth that the account, from an American newspaper, was exaggerated. Hutchinson thought 'there appeared a degree of that apathy which I think Lord North has a great deal of'. When confirmation came in Gage's official report on 10 June North and his cabinet colleagues recognized that war had begun, and only Dartmouth showed reluctance to take 'vigorous' measures.[39] The cabinet busied itself with military preparations, especially after news came on 25 July of the battle of Bunker Hill, where Gage's army suffered over 1,000 casualties in a pyrrhic victory. North commented to George III the next day that 'the war is now grown to such a height that it must be treated as a foreign war, and that every expedient which would be used in the latter case should be applied in the former.'[40] It did not need the King's pressure to galvanize the administration into action. Already steps had been taken to hire soldiers from German states and, without success, from Russia: and in late July and early August much attention was given to the drafting of a Proclamation of Rebellion. This was formally issued on 23 August, even though unofficial news had come of the 'Olive Branch Petition' from Congress, asking for a colonial Magna Carta and offering to submit to trade regulation by Britain.

The ministry subsequently decided to ignore the petition on the technical ground that the Crown could not recognize the existence of such a body as the Congress. This intransigence alienated some administration supporters in Britain, where it was widely known that the petition had been the result of a compromise whereby the American radicals had given way to advocates of conciliation. Grafton was one who thought it provided the last chance of preventing a colonial declaration of independence. He spoke against administration policy at the beginning of the next parliamentary session in October, and was promptly asked to surrender the Privy Seal. Another former cabinet minister who opposed the American war was General Conway, hitherto an unreliable supporter of government: their behaviour, and the reluctance of some who remained in office to become too closely involved in the conduct of the war signified a trend of opinion that was as yet of little importance. The great majority of government supporters, officeholders and independents alike, were to support the American war until its military failure became apparent. But Grafton's resignation fortuitously precipitated a brief ministerial crisis.

Dartmouth had defended the ministry's American policy in debate, but he had no desire to direct a war against the colonies. Neither did he wish to desert North, and he therefore asked to succeed Grafton. His request led to a situation that tested North's tact and ingenuity. Weymouth, then holding the court sinecure of Groom of the Stole, already had a promise of any important office that should become vacant. Failure to give him the Privy Seal would alienate him and offend Gower and other former Bedfordites. George III therefore suggested that an offer he deemed equal to the Privy Seal should be made to Dartmouth, Weymouth's post but with a seat in the cabinet. Dartmouth refused, and a worried North told the King that the administration might collapse unless both Dartmouth and Weymouth could be satisfied. North had himself meanwhile complicated the problem by a premature offer of Dartmouth's post to Lord George Germain.

There had been for some time a general expectation that Germain would join the ministry. The former Lord George Sackville court-martialled after the battle of Minden in 1759, Germain had long since completed his political rehabilitation and made a name as an able and effective speaker in the Commons. He had supported the administration's American policy in 1774 and 1775 and had recently been in touch with Suffolk and other former Grenvillites in the administration. Germain was a forceful advocate of the policy of bringing America to submission. He enjoyed a reputation for ad-ministrative efficiency. But the prospect of his front-bench assistance in debate may have been the chief reason for North's offer: Lady North commented to Lord Guilford that 'it will be a great ease to him to have a responsible person in the House of Commons, for the three Secretaries being all in the House of Lords made his situation in the House of Commons more disagreeable'.[41]

The King promised North every assistance in this predicament: 'You are my sheet anchor and your ease and comfort I shall in the whole transaction try to secure.' Within a day North had devised what he thought to be the solution. He persuaded Southern Secretary Rochford, then in a bad state of health, to resign on promise of certain inducements, notably an additional pension of £2,500, so that his post could be offered to Dartmouth or Weymouth. Dartmouth refused this promotion to a more senior office, telling North that he was determined either to have the Privy Seal or to retain his present office. He was quite willing to resign altogether, but realized that this would weaken his step-brother's position in the cabinet, a point made by North himself to a King angry at Dart-mouth's unexpected obduracy. It was Weymouth who agreed to give way: although valuing the American Secretaryship now more highly than he had done in 1772, he agreed to accept Rochford's office instead.[42] The whole episode ended with the ministry stronger. Both Bedfordites and Grenvillites were satisfied. North still had Dartmouth at his side in the cabinet, and Germain was a valuable acquisition in both debate and administration. But the political balance of the cabinet had been tilted still more towards the hard-liners at a time when North was making a final effort to conciliate America.

North was now convinced that peace could only be won by coer-cion, and on 20 October had rejected as unrealistic a plea by Grafton for the cessation of hostilities:[43]

Your humble servant, and I believe I may add His Majesty's other counsellors, still remain ready to agree with any province in

D

America upon the footing of the resolution of the House of Commons of the 27th February last: but the leaders of the rebellion in the colonies plainly declare themselves not satisfied with those conditions and manifestly aim at a total independence. Against this we propose to exert ourselves using every species of force to reduce them; but authorising at the same time either the Commander in Chief or some other Commissioner to proclaim immediately peace and pardon, and to restore all the privileges of trade to any colonies upon its submission. Authority will likewise be given to settle the question of taxation for the future upon the plan held forth last year; and to put every other matter now in dispute between them and this country in a course of accommodation. Till the provinces have made some submission, it will be in vain to hope that they will come into any reasonable terms, and I am afraid that declaring a cessation of arms at this time would establish that independence which the leaders of the faction in America have always intended, and which they now almost openly avow.

This was North's assessment of the American situation, and the basis of his policy. He won the approval of his colleagues for the Peace Commission only by portraying the scheme as a means of accelerating colonial submission, and there remained in some quarters the belief that North's conciliation was intended merely to placate parliamentary criticism: Treasury Lord Charles Cornwall commented at the end of October that North was 'too much afraid of the opposition. All the independent landed interest of the kingdom vote with government, in what relates to America.'[44] Such doubts as to his sincerity do scant justice to North, whose idea of a Peace Commission was a practical extension of his policy earlier in the year. The King's Speech at the beginning of the new parliamentary session on 26 October mentioned the proposed Commission, but the trend of ministerial opinion was shown by the open and unwise accusation that the colonies were aiming at independence. In the debate North declared that the administration meant 'to send a powerful sea and land force to America, and at the same time to accompany them with offers of mercy upon a proper submission': and he won a 278 to 108 vote of support for this policy.[45]

Military preparations fell to the executive, and the chief measure of legislation was a Prohibitory Bill, to stop all colonial trade by the seizure of American shipping. North secured the inclusion of a clause to authorize George III to appoint a Peace Commission, and when he introduced the bill in the Commons on 20 November reiterated his willingness to abandon taxation of any colony that agreed to pay the cost of its government and defence. At the second reading of the bill on 1 December he said that any such colony would not have to make a general acknowledgement of Parliament's supremacy.[46] But that was as far as North was prepared to go. Throughout all the debates of the session on America he consistently rejected the opposition remedy of a total repeal of all colonial legislation since 1763. That would not do, he said, because the authority of Parliament was challenged in America and would first have to be established.

North's initiative for conciliation was once again overtaken by events. The Prohibitory Act, authorizing the dispatch of the Peace Commission, was law before the end of 1775; and by February 1776 the new naval Commander-in-Chief Lord Howe and his brother General Howe, now the army commander, had been named joint Commissioners. But there followed a long delay while Germain led an attempt within the ministry to prevent any negotiation until the colonies had made formal acknowledgement of Parliament's right to legislate for them. North had to agree to a compromise that while discussions could begin without such an admission there could be no peace until it had been made.[47] This and other stipulations effectively destroyed North's faint hopes of being able to negotiate a settlement instead of having to win a war. The colonists had discussed and rejected the proposals before Lord Howe arrived in New York on 12 July: and eight days earlier the colonial Declaration of Independence had created a barrier to all meaningful negotiations.

Where does North stand in relation to the American Revolution? The image of a conciliatory moderate he later tried to create is only part of the story, and the less important part. Right up until the end of 1774 North was the foremost advocate of colonial taxation in theory and practice, and he was personally involved in the coercive legislation of that year that drove the Americans to resist. It was too late in the day when he perceived the danger of a civil war with the colonies, and made his unsuccessful attempts to avert that calamity. It is of course to North's credit that he did at least try to avoid the conflict which seemed almost to be welcomed by British majority opinion, from the throne down to the man in the street. The political situation in Britain made reconciliation impossible. North could never have obtained cabinet and parliamentary approval to offer the colonies more than he did. That left a gap that could not be bridged, formal rights of taxation and actual powers of legislation claimed by Britain and denied by America: a gap revealed, for example, by comparison of North's conciliatory proposals of 1775 with the minimum demands even of the most loyalist colony, New York. Undoubtedly he was handicapped in his attempts at conciliation by the attitude of his ministerial colleagues and by the state of parliamentary opinion on America. But these limitations on his freedom of action cannot hide the fact that North never envisaged the sweeping concessions that would alone have pacified the colonies. He readily settled for the sword rather than the olive branch. If the policy of 1774 sought to establish Parliamentary sovereignty through legislation, that of 1775 was characterized by a determination to enforce colonial subordination by resort to arms if necessary. North's conduct does not match his subsequent portrayal of himself as a potential saviour of the First British Empire thwarted by a bellicose Parliament and nation.

5

THE AMERICAN WAR
1775–82

That his ministry involved Britain in a war
with her own colonies is only part of the traditional charge against
North: that his administration was so incompetent as to lose this
contest has strengthened the historical condemnation of him, the
failure appearing the more reprehensible as the only British defeat in
recent centuries. Criticism of the North ministry, both contemporary
and historical, has embraced not only the mismanagement of the war
itself but also the alleged prior neglect of the navy and a foreign
policy that had left Britain isolated. These last two accusations have
both been demolished by recent scholarship, and neither is directly
a charge against North himself; but some consideration of them is

relevant to any assessment of North's role as Prime Minister and his share of responsibility for the American disaster.

The basic assumption behind any criticism of British foreign policy at this time is that defeat in the War of American Independence could have been prevented if there had been allies against France.[1] In the years after 1763 Britain did seek an ally, but the field among the great powers was confined to Russia. Spain was now permanently linked to France by Bourbon family compacts. Austria had become a French ally in 1756, and saw no advantage in returning to the old Grand Alliance with Britain that had broken down in mid-century. Frederick II of Prussia was now hostile after his desertion in the Seven Years' War. Negotiations with Catherine II went on for a decade, and Russia gained much from British friendship, notably help in the transfer of the Russian navy from the Baltic to the Mediterranean that resulted in the annihilation of the Turkish fleet off Asia Minor in July 1770. The next month Weymouth offered to negotiate a peace guaranteeing the Russian acquisitions in the Balkans if a Treaty of Alliance would include Russian help against attacks on British possessions in America and India. Russia refused this offer, and without such a provision Britain was not prepared to pay the price Russia asked successively of naval help against Turkey, financial subsidies to Denmark and Sweden, and finally a guarantee of the territories acquired by Russia in the First Partition of Poland in 1772.

That event served to spark off new thinking about British foreign policy, as the realization dawned that Britain and Russia had little in common and that France shared the same apprehensions as Britain about the situation in eastern Europe. The possibility of an Anglo–French *rapprochement* was increased by the Swedish Revolution later that year, a *coup d'état* in August 1772 by the new pro-French King Gustav III. He then overthrew the rule af the so-called 'Cap' party, the faction hitherto supported by Russian and British diplomacy; and there suddenly appeared the spectre of a new European war, as Gustav appealed to France for help against the anticipated Russian attack.* British intervention successfully prevented a war. Russia was warned that if one occurred a French fleet would be allowed into the Baltic, and France was told not to attack the vulnerable Russian position in the Mediterranean. Once again,

---

* Foreign policy was not Lord North's province, but it does seem extraordinary that he should be so unaware of the danger that at this very time he asked Sandwich to cut the naval estimates and had to be reminded of the international crisis. *Sandwich Papers*, 1, 20–24.

as in the Falkland Islands dispute of 1770, the mere threat of the British navy sufficed to prevent a war. But the North ministry reaped no reward from this diplomatic triumph. The quest for a Russian alliance had been abandoned, and popular prejudice in Britain rendered impossible the one with France fleetingly and vaguely contemplated by the ministry. The Swedish crisis had led Britain into secret negotiations with France, a move certainly sanctioned by North himself in the early months of 1773. Further reflection must have shown the sterility of any such policy, for Parliament would not tolerate any suggestion of a French alliance. The potential diplomatic revolution was still-born, and in 1774 Vergennes came to power in France with the Choiseul policy of a war of revenge on Britain: but if the premiss that France was an inveterate enemy was seemingly confirmed by the War of American Independence it had not been valid in the early 1770s.

British foreign policy at this time cannot be condemned as a failure to obtain an ally: it was rather a decision not to seek one on unfavourable terms. There was always the realization that Britain might have to face a war against France and Spain together: but the assumption was that a navy superior to their combined fleets would be better security than the prospect of help from Russia or any other ally, and it was well-founded. The Russian alliance that might have been obtained at a price could have done little to help Britain against the Bourbon Powers with Germany neutralized at the joint insistence of Austria and Prussia. Perhaps the 20,000 Russian soldiers requested as mercenaries in 1775 would not have been refused if Russia had been a formal ally: but the only certain consequence of British isolation was the League of Armed Neutrality organized by Russia in 1780 against Britain's naval blockade of her enemies, and that did not cause serious difficulties.

The basic calculation proved wrong only because Britain's customary command of the sea was to be destroyed by the unforeseen strain of the American situation. This consequence has often overshadowed the fact that the precaution of matching European naval strength had been taken. The man responsible for this achievement was Sandwich.[2] He inherited a fleet that on paper contained 86 ships of the line in 1771, but by the next year he was claiming that only 15 of them were 'fit for the sea': certainly by 1779 only 17 of the 43 still in service had not needed major repairs. Yet by then the fleet was some 100 ships, the same size as in 1759, the famous 'year of victories'. North had perceived in 1770 that Sandwich was the right man for the Admiralty, but apart from his appointment can take little credit for the state of the navy. On the contrary, North was always seeking to curb naval expenditure in his general search for financial economies, and in 1772 he proposed to reduce the active peacetime fleet from 20 to 16 ships, arguing that improvement of the national credit by economy and debt repayment would strengthen Britain's financial position in any future war: 'Great peace establishments will, if we do not take care, prove our ruin: we shall fail, at the long run, by exhausting in times of tranquillity those resources upon which we are to depend in time of war.'[3] Sandwich convinced the cabinet that such a reduction would be dangerous, and from 1776 he secured a gradual increase in the fleet by producing evidence of French and Spanish naval preparations. North agreed with the principle of matching French re-armaments, and in 1777 asked his own military advisers to consider methods of countering possible French invasion plans. Once North saw the danger to national security he cast aside all thoughts of naval economy and involved himself in detailed discussions on naval requirements.[4]

The international policy of the North ministry before the American War cannot be deemed as anything other than a success. National prestige had been upheld during the two crises of the Falkland Islands and the Swedish Revolution. Such episodes confirmed the wisdom of acting without the encumbrance of an ally. North's attempt to reduce the number of ships in 1772 would seem a damning indictment of him in retrospect, but it may not be fanciful to link it with the hopes at that time of Anglo–French friendship. There was never any abandonment of the decision to put faith in the British navy rather than a continental ally.

When the soundness of this judgement was invalidated by the alliance of colonial rebels with European enemies the North ministry did not lack diplomatic initiative. After France in 1778 and Spain in 1779 had entered the war, considerable efforts were made to secure Spanish neutrality and a Russian alliance. An attempt to buy off Spain through the cession of Gibraltar was approved by North but vetoed by the cabinet. An approach to Russia in 1779 failed, and was followed the next year by the League of Armed Neutrality. The North ministry, misled by envoy James Harris at St Petersburg, then made an offer of Britain's Mediterranean naval base of Minorca, a move rejected by Catherine II early in 1781.[5] But this search for Russian help in the unique circumstances of the American War does not justify condemnation of North's administration for its peacetime policy of 'splendid isolation'.

Lord North has always borne the historical responsibility for the loss of America, but he was not the man who conducted the war. A biography of North is therefore the place only for an assessment of his personal contribution, not for the whole story of the American conflict. North's role in the war was threefold. His political function as head of the ministry was to hold the administration together and to act as chief spokesman in the Commons, with the task of explaining and defending government policy there.* Secondly he was head of the Treasury, the department responsible for both national finance and the arrangements for supplying the British army overseas. Thirdly he was first minister in a cabinet which decided strategy and the organisation of the war effort. All these activities comprised a superhuman task when things were not going well, as North complained to George III in 1778.[6]

> Lord North thinks it his duty to represent to his Majesty that to perform the duties of the Treasury, to attend the House of Commons at the rate of three long days a week, to see the numbers of persons who have daily business with the First Lord of the Treasury, and to give all thought to the principal measures of government in this very alarming crisis is enough to employ the greatest man of business, and the most consummate statesman that ever existed, and is infinitely more than Lord North can undertake.

The immense burden of work North shouldered at the Treasury itself was reflected in his attendance at the Treasury Board. From the beginning of 1775 until his resignation in 1782 North missed only 23 of 670 formal Board meetings. Often this was routine business undertaken because of the poor attendance of his junior colleagues: Treasury Secretary John Robinson complained in 1779 that North was prevented from giving attention to more important subjects because 'he was kept so employed in Treasury matters which might be done by other Lords, but that he had no Lord to sit with him'.[7] The extra strain on the Treasury was caused by the department's responsibility for such additional tasks as organizing and arranging the continuous supply of food and drink, fuel and money, for the British army overseas and for the raising and financing of massive loans.

Both these functions were to incur contemporary accusations that have long sullied North's reputation. The attacks concerned his countenance of political corruption, and the costly incompetence of his administration in the assignment of war contracts and the floating of financial loans. These changes would have received less attention from contemporaries and historians but for the twin

---

* This political story is told in the next chapter.

circumstances of an eloquent opposition and an unsuccessful war. They were unfair, but not altogether unfounded. The time-hallowed method of obtaining both army supplies and financial loans by private negotiation was obviously open to the charge of undue political influence. Mistakes were made, and not all of North's associates had clean hands, although his own personal integrity was never in question. Yet realization has now come that North's record at the Treasury serves to enhance and not diminish his reputation. The maintenance of supply to the British army in America was a successful operation, in the face of immense physical and organizational problems. Money was found for the war by loans, and taxes contrived to service them. And in the midst of all these labours North still found time to consider and evolve improvements in the conduct of business by the Treasury, even though their implementation had to be left to his successors.

It was in the allocation of army supply contracts, negotiated privately with merchants and bankers, that the North ministry faced repeated charges of extravagance and corruption.[8] Circumstances seemed to provide grounds for such accusations. The contracts were usually assigned by North's patronage Secretary to the Treasury, John Robinson, though North himself was closely involved in decisions on them and responsible for their political defence in the House of Commons. Many of the contractors made large fortunes during the war, and of the forty-six contractors employed between 1775 and 1782 eighteen were M.P.s and eighteen more had some connexion with M.P.s. The vociferous criticism of the parliamentary opposition generated the suspicion that the disposal of these contracts formed part of ministerial patronage by yielding exorbitant profits to favoured applicants with parliamentary connexions. So strong was this assumption that after North's fall his critics secured the passage of legislation debarring government contractors from sitting in Parliament, the so-called Clerke's Act of 1782. Recent interpretations take a less cynical view of the contracting system. The patronage element involved in the situation was rather the simple one of giving business to the administration's friends than the deliberate bestowal of unduly lucrative contracts. Many of the contractors would have given political support to North without such inducements; and the man over whose contracts North's critics made the greatest noise, Richard Atkinson, was not an M.P. at all.

North and Robinson were soon under no illusions about the practical and political disadvantages of their contracting methods, but they could see no better alternative. The field of choice was limited, for only a few large firms could support overseas contracts. If the ministry had adopted the system of open competitive tendering advocated by North's opponents the result might easily have been the failure of successful bidders to supply the contracted provisions and the risk of consequent military disasters: reliability had to be taken into account as well as cost. There is no doubt that Treasury negligence did lead to high profits on provisioning contracts during the early years of the war, but improvements were soon made in the allocation and supervision of contract business under the twin spurs of parliamentary criticism of excessive contracting profits and the growing realization by the administration that the war would be long and expensive. On 15 May 1777 Barré asserted in the Commons that Atkinson had been given a contract to supply rum to the army in America at 5s. 3d. a gallon when other merchants thought 3s. 6d. a favourable price. North's defence of the contract confused sterling and local currency to such an extent that he calculated the total cost of supplying rum to be 5s. 11d., and therefore claimed with jovial humour that the Treasury had made a good bargain. Barré tartly rejoined that Atkinson must be 'the greatest idiot in the whole contracting world'. North then admitted his error, and Dunning commented that the only thing clear about the whole transaction was North's 'perfect ignorance'.[9] This parliamentary attack led to a Treasury investigation and a reduction in contract prices after the discovery that the Navy Victualling Board had supplied inaccurate information. North and Robinson, subjected to frequent criticism in Parliament and the press, gradually effected vast improvements by comparative pricing, efficient accounting, and better quality control. By 1780 the profit on supply contracts was down from 15 or 20 per cent to about 10 per cent.

All wars breed profiteers, and criticism of the Treasury contract system meets the practical answer that it worked, despite problems of punctuality and storage. The war was not lost because of administrative defects, and the British army never ran into serious supply problems. From the first the Treasury kept a close eye on the detailed working of the system, as by an order of 1776 that the barrels used for packaging food should be secured by four metal hoops instead of two. But except in the financial terms of contracts there was little scope for improvements: for there always remained the difficulty of the indirect chain of command, the lack of control over the persons actually supplying the commodities.

Until 1779 the Treasury also shouldered the practical responsibility for transporting the army provisions to America, since the Admiralty refused to undertake the problem of supplying some 30,000 men at a distance of 3,000 miles in the face of hostile privateering. It was one outside the Treasury's experience, and the department adopted the practice of sending not convoys but single armed ships. The device proved very successful: it incurred few losses, ensured greater regularity, and obviated one duty for naval ships. The magnitude of the task was such that the Treasury was employing 115 ships in 1778, and the whole operation has been acclaimed 'a great logistical and administrative achievement' by the historian of British shipping in the war.[10] But it was conducted before French and Spanish intervention made the seas more unsafe, and the transfer of the function to the Navy Board early in 1779 was in this respect timely.

A more familiar task for the Treasury was the financing of the war. North, as Chancellor of the Exchequer, had no chance of meeting more than a small proportion of wartime expenditure out of current revenues. These yielded around £7,000,000, whereas by 1780 war costs had gradually raised annual government spending to over £20,000,000. North had to borrow the difference each year, and devise taxation to meet the additional-interest burden. Herein lies one of the gravest charges against North's ability as a minister.[11]

It was long a historical commonplace that North's wartime finance proved costly and inefficient, increasing the National Debt out of all proportion to the sums of money actually borrowed. Such an assumption overlooks the growing difficulty North encountered in borrowing money when government stock prices were depressed by an expensive and unsuccessful war: the price of 3 per cent stock fell from 86 in 1776 to 54 in 1782. It also does scant justice to North's financial ingenuity. He attempted to keep both the interest and the borrowed capital as low as possible, seeking to achieve these conflicting objectives by astute use of dated annuities and by continued exploitation of the public demand for lottery tickets; the exclusive privilege of buying them was now given to subscribers to government loans.

North had a choice of three methods of raising a loan. An open subscription he never attempted because the risk of failure made it too hazardous in wartime, so he told M.P.s in 1779: the difficulty lay in calculating an offer price in a fluctuating market that would raise the money required yet would not be too generous a bargain for subscribers. Nor did North employ the device of secret tender bidding until the last year of his ministry. The method he adopted was the customary one of private negotiations with a number of individuals.

This allowed scope for bargaining, but involved the political disadvantage that the Chancellor of the Exchequer or his Treasury minions might be accused of using loan subscriptions as a form of political corruption. It worked well for the first few years of the war, and that was the important point for North, who reminded George III in 1778 that 'the power of borrowing has been hitherto the principal source of the greatness and weight of Great Britain'.[12]

In 1776 North needed to borrow £2,000,000. This he did by issuing £2,135,000 of 3 per cent stock, the premium being rendered more attractive by a lottery device whereby each £100 brought the subscriber £77 10s. of stock and three £11 10s. lottery tickets. North had taken advantage of the 'lottery mania' to make a good bargain for the public, since with the market price of 3 per cent stock at 86 it would have cost £2,325,000 to raise the loan in orthodox fashion: but he was not able to repeat the coup as market conditions got more difficult. In 1777 North needed to borrow £5,000,000. With the price of 3 per cent stock now at 80 he issued the loan in 4 per cent stock, which was to yield 4½ per cent for the first ten years only: and subscribers had the option of buying one £10 lottery ticket for every £100 of stock. Many subscribers to the 1777 loan made an overall loss, and next year, in the aftermath of Saratoga, North was obliged to offer terms that he admitted to be generous, arguing that he did not dare risk the failure of the subscription to provide the money required. With 3 per cent stock currently standing at 66, North issued the £6,000,000 he needed in that stock but with an extra 2½ per cent interest for the first thirty years. This added 35 to the value of the stock, so he told the Commons, and there was the further inducement of being allowed to buy £10 lottery tickets at the rate of eight for every £1,000 subscribed. In 1779 North told M.P.s that he had experienced great difficulty in negotiating a loan, and had raised £7,000,000 by issuing a 3 per cent stock that carried an additional 3¾ per cent interest for twenty-nine years, with the *douceur* of purchasing seven lottery tickets for every £1,000 subscribed. 1780 saw North boasting of a better bargain. Needing to borrow £12,000,000, he had obtained par for a 4 per cent stock carrying an additional interest of £1 16s. 3d. for eighty years, with the bonus of buying four lottery tickets for every £1,000 subscribed. Until 1780 North's loan finance was an undoubted success. Despite the steady fall of the 3 per cent stock to a market price of 60 he had contrived to issue new 3 and 4 per cent stock at par by the two devices of lottery tickets affording an immediate cash bonus to subscribers who wished to resell and the offer of higher interest for limited periods.

The damage to North's financial reputation came with the loan of 1781. He told the Commons that the bad state of government funds had forced him into a disadvantageous bargain: 3 per cent stock was at 59, and lenders were not prepared to risk even this market price in case it fell still lower. The final terms had been settled at a meeting of some thirty leading applicants, including representatives of the Bank of England and the East India Company. Each subscriber of £100 was to be allotted £150 of 3 per cent stock and £25 of 4 per cent stock, and have the right to buy four lottery tickets for each £1,000 lent. North admitted that this method would increase the capital debt by £21,000,000 for the loan of the £12,000,000 required, but 'upon the whole considered this the cheapest mode of borrowing money'. He now frankly told the House that popular alarm about the size of the National Debt had hitherto led him to borrow on a different principle: but 'it had always been his opinion, that the best way of making a loan, was by increasing the capital, and to raise the money at as low an interest as possible, because it was the interest that the people were burdened with paying off, and not the capital'. Opposition M.P.s seized on this implicit admission that the National Debt would never be repaid, and the loan was the subject of several heated debates. Charles Fox attacked North for changing his methods, but opposition criticism mainly concerned alleged corruption. Fox claimed that the profit would be £900,000 and that this would go to M.P.s and other ministerial supporters: on Budget Day a motion to cancel the lottery altogether was proposed, and defeated by 169 votes to 111. Further charges of partiality followed publication of the list of subscribers. Opposition M.P.s said that respectable gentlemen and former subscribers had got little or nothing, while most of the loan went to favourites of the minister. Fox denounced the attitude of some M.P.s as shameful: 'It was such a conduct as the noble lord in the blue ribbon would not be guilty of himself, however much he might encourage it in others.'

A great increase in the number of applicants, from 240 in 1778 to 1145 in 1781, had made the allocation of loan stock a difficult and protracted task. It had been made not by North or his Secretaries to the Treasury but by the permanent staff of the Treasury, and it was matter for further scandal that Treasury clerks had allotted stock to themselves. North assured the House that no applications had been accepted after the terms were decided, and that he had ordered the distribution to be made with impartiality: but, although he deemed it abuse and misrepresentation, the volume of complaint led North to adopt a different method for what was to prove his last loan.

In 1782 he needed to raise £13,500,000. In January a syndicate of four, headed by M.P. Thomas Harley and including contractor Richard Atkinson and the royal banker Henry Drummond, offered to take either £6,000,000 or the whole loan at a discount of 2 per cent. The next month North received a second offer from a consortium led by banker M.P. Abel Smith. Both groups were composed of administration supporters and neither knew the terms proposed by the other. North consulted various financiers, including the Governor of the Bank of England: all agreed that the first proposal was the more acceptable, and more favourable indeed than the bargain of 1781, even though the price of stock was lower still. The terms North announced to the House were that each subscriber of £100 would receive £100 of 3 per cent stock, £50 of 4 per cent stock, and an annuity of 17s. 6d. for seventy-eight years, plus the right to purchase lottery tickets at the rate of three for every £1,000 subscribed. North had insisted that the whole loan should be contracted for, and the invidious task of distributing the loan among the 2,469 applicants who had offered £73,000,000 was left to the successful bidders, with the stipulation that no M.P. was to receive more than £10,000 worth of stock. Although opposition complaints were voiced that the new system was a means of secret influence North had hit upon the method that his successors were to adopt and improve: competitive secret offers divorced the allotment of loans from political implications.

In his seven wartime loan operations North had raised £57,500,000, at the cost of increasing the funded National Debt by just over £75,000,000. The total would undoubtedly have been significantly higher but for North's clever use of annuities and lotteries: the annuity payments would begin to stop from 1787, and by 1808 60 per cent of them would have ended. The total annual interest burden of his war loans, including these dated payments, amounted to £3,240,000, having risen from £64,000 in 1776 to £793,000 in 1782. The devising of extra annual taxation to pay these costs had tested North's ingenuity to the utmost.

In 1777 North told the Commons the principles he meant to adopt. He would throw the cost 'as much as possible on the opulent; or, in other words . . . tax property instead of labour'. He would tax not trade and manufacturing, nor 'the lower part of the community', but 'property and the luxuries of life'. He practised these ideas as long as possible, omitting such items as candles and leather from the blanket surcharges in customs and excise duties levied in 1779 and 1781. Most of his new taxes fell on those best able to pay. Five times he imposed higher stamp duties of various kinds. There were taxes on carriages and stage-coaches in 1776; taxes on auctions and male servants in 1777; a legacy duty in 1780, when North told M.P.s he had been thinking of a death duty; and an entertainment duty in 1782, bitterly opposed by the playright M.P. Richard Sheridan. In the last years of the war North had to cast his net wider. Nearly the whole of his extra tax burden in 1780 fell on the import or production of alcohol, which was consumed by rich and poor alike: and with reluctance he imposed taxes on some necessities of life; extra salt taxes in 1780 and 1782, a sugar duty in 1781, and in 1782 a tax on soap, which, he said, was 'not consumed in large quantities by the poor'.

North always sought to raise slightly more taxation than he calculated to be necessary, but this precaution did not prevent a tax deficit. He encountered the problem of tax evasion with his servants tax of 1777 and above all over his house tax of 1778, his one attempt to find a productive new source of revenue. Here North was influenced by the ideas of Adam Smith, an advocate of direct taxation, who in 1778 was appointed to the Scottish Customs Board as an acknowledgement of his value to the Treasury in devising new sources of revenue. The house tax was intended to correct the defects of the land tax, which was too narrowly based to tap the nation's wealth. Levied at 6d. in £1 on houses of rents from £5 to £50, and at 1s. on houses over £50, the tax should have yielded £260,000 a year. But an inefficient system of assessment and collection, compounded by fraudulent evasion, resulted in a yield of under £100,000 in the first year: it remained deficient even afterwards, and North had to admit that it was not so easy to assess and collect as the analogous window tax. North also encountered evasion in his post-chaise tax of that year, and the accumulated tax deficit by 1781 was £639,000 for the previous four years. It was this difficulty encountered with new taxes, North told the Commons, that led him to fall back on the safe method of increasing such older sources of revenue as the customs and excise duties and the stamp duties.

If North could do little about the revenue-collecting machinery in the country, he did attempt to improve it at the centre of government. His long experience at the Treasury and Exchequer had made him painfully aware of the costly inefficiency of a system of revenue in which many taxes and duties were appropriated to such purposes as servicing different parts of the National Debt: and he ordered the

Customs, Excise and Stamp Boards to prepare schemes for the
consolidation of revenue, plans begun in 1777 but still incomplete at
his resignation. A more important foundation laid by North for the
administrative reforms of his successors was his Commission on the
Public Accounts, established in 1780. The opposition was demanding
a Parliamentary Committee of Accounts, with the intention of
blaming the ministry for faults and abuses that had long existed.
North sidestepped this particular attack by proposing on 2 March a
statutory Commission with powers to send for all documents and
to examine witnesses on oath, advantages denied to a House of
Commons Committee. The ensuing Act, drafted by Charles Jenkinson, appointed six named commissioners to examine the public
accounts, report defects and suggest improvements: these men were
not politicians but professional experts like bankers and lawyers.
The creation of the Commission was not merely an act of political
expediency. North's concern with administrative efficiency had
earlier been demonstrated by a Treasury Board Minute of 22
February 1776 declaring that the criterion for future promotions
within the department should be not seniority but ability, care and
diligence. He had become ever more reluctant to reward electoral
and political services with sinecures and pensions. And while he was
minister he made positive efforts to implement the recommendations
of the Commission.

Only six of the fifteen reports made by the Commission over a
period of seven years were submitted before North left office. The
sole parliamentary discussion of the subject initiated by North took
place on 10 May 1781, over the first four reports.[13] North said, and
his claim is confirmed by Treasury papers, that he had consulted
departments criticized in the reports: but he usually took at face
value department statements that many of the proposed changes
were 'impracticable'. North, for example, accepted the principle of
consolidating revenue offices, but in practice consolidated only two
minor ones, those for hackney coaches and hawkers and pedlars,
thereby saving a mere £300. The worst abuses condemned in these
early reports were the retention by officials of taxes that had been
collected, notably by receivers of the land tax; and the practice of
government accountants, like the Navy Treasurers and Army
Paymasters-General, of retaining official balances in their private
possession until their accounts had been passed by the Exchequer,
whose 'old forms and regulations' were blamed by North for the
inordinate delays that often lasted a decade or more. He therefore
introduced legislation to deal with these matters: financial penalties

would be imposed on land-tax receivers who did not pay over their money within a specified time-limit; and the excuse of government accountants was to be removed by a bill giving them parliamentary security for money handed over before audit. The legislation of 1781 was ineffective, the land-tax proposal never even reaching the statute book: but North was afterwards too involved in the final political crisis of his ministry to take any further step.

With his belief in direct taxation and his frank realization that the National Debt would never be paid off, North was a finance minister of the future rather than the past. Practical competence complemented this perception. Faced with an obsolete system of public finance, he had sought new ways of taxation, designed to hit those best able to pay: and his ingenuity had kept going the traditional method of raising wartime loans on an altogether unprecedented scale in very difficult market conditions. But he had aimed to do more than merely make the existing system work. He intended to change it, and the implications of the various initiatives that he took were far-reaching: the abandonment of the age-old principle of the personal responsibility of an office-holder for any public funds passing through his hands; effective audit of public accounts instead of the largely formal processes of the Exchequer; and consolidation both of the sources of national revenue and of the machinery for collecting it. There is good reason to think that North would have begun a major overhaul of the financial machinery of the central government if he had remained in office for a few more years, and it is indeed remarkable that he should have been thinking of such matters at all during the American War. Such successors as Shelburne and Pitt carried out many of the ideas floated by North, and made use of the information he had ordered to be collected: their biographers have rightly paid tribute to North as a capable and far-sighted Chancellor of the Exchequer.[14]

But the gravamen of the charge concerning North's responsibility for defeat in the American War concerns his lack of leadership as Prime Minister, not alleged errors of administration at the Treasury. That is to misunderstand his role. Certainly, in theory, responsibility for the direction of the war lay with the cabinet of which he was head. North himself sometimes enunciated the doctrine of collective cabinet responsibility in the Commons, as on 14 December 1778 and 3 March 1779; and Sandwich made this note in an undated memorandum: 'Every expedition in regard to its destination, object, force, and number of ships, is planned by the Cabinet, and is the result of the collective wisdom of all his Majesty's confidential ministers.'[15]

Practice differed from theory, for the North ministry was one of government by departments. Individual ministers formulated policies appertaining to their spheres of responsibility and sought cabinet approval for them. The war minister was American Secretary Lord George Germain. In the first months of each year he prepared plans for the forthcoming campaigns and secured cabinet endorsement of them. A competent and efficient departmental head, Germain lacked the prestige, popularity and authority that had enabled the Elder Pitt in the Seven Years' War to weld the British government into a military machine. His efforts were clogged by bureaucratic inefficiency, and he was confronted with military and naval commanders who for political or other reasons could not be kept in order. Sandwich at the Admiralty was over-cautious, concerned to preserve the fleet and his own reputation. A stronger Prime Minister might have secured better cooperation between Germain and Sandwich by knocking their heads together. North was well aware that the lack of cohesion in the conduct of the war reflected on himself as Prime Minister, and it was a point he frequently urged on the King from 1778 onwards. His failure of political leadership in the closing years of the war was a shortcoming made much of by contemporaries and historians; but it had little adverse effect on the conduct of the war. When everything is said that can be said about the political weaknesses of the North ministry, they were not a significant cause in themselves of the British failure in the war.

If North would have received hardly more credit for victory than Newcastle did in the Seven Years' War, so can his contribution to defeat be deemed small. The story of his personal role in the evolution of strategy and detailed tactical planning of campaigns is soon told, for it was seldom distinctive. It must be assumed that he concurred in all cabinet decisions on policy unless there is evidence to the contrary, but he already carried such a burden of parliamentary duties and Treasury work that he could give the war little attention, and his personal efforts seem to have been directed rather to obtaining an end to the fighting than to securing a vigorous prosecution of the war. There are occasional glimpses of his own actions, as in December 1775, when he was reluctantly drawn in to assist Germain in the planning of the relief force for Quebec that was to save Canada the next year. North was seldom so directly involved in military affairs, and there is even considerable doubt as to how far he was concerned in the most fateful decision of the war: approval of the 1777 campaign. He did attend the cabinet meeting that on 24 February appointed Burgoyne commander of the army that was to advance south from Canada, but a bad cold worsened the next day and he was confined to his house for some weeks: he was unable to go to the Treasury or the House of Commons, and may not have been at cabinet while the final strategic planning was being completed.[16] It is in any case arguable how far the ministry was responsible for the disaster. The cabinet's simultaneous approval of Burgoyne's march from Canada and Howe's attack on Philadelphia was given on the assumption that Howe would complete his Pennsylvania campaign in time to assist Burgoyne if necessary; and it was with justifiable misgivings that the administration learned during the summer that Howe would be too late to be able to do so. Nor can the ministry be blamed for failure to realize the hazards of Burgoyne's march from Canada when the generals in America were confident of its success. But however defensible the government decision may have been, Burgoyne's surrender at Saratoga in October was a disaster for which the cabinet had to bear the political responsibility. It far outweighed Howe's capture of Philadelphia and led to a revised war strategy, a ministerial crisis, and the first significant parliamentary attacks on the conduct of the war.*

The effect on North himself was a renewal of his attempts at conciliation. He had already been searching for an end to hostilities when the war news still seemed favourable, and on 4 November, before news of Saratoga, made this comment about the draft of the King's Speech for the new parliamentary session: 'How shall we mention America? Shall we be very stout? Or shall we take advantage of the flourishing state of our affairs to get out of this d—d war and hold a moderate language?'[17] The remark was made to William Eden, Suffolk's Under-Secretary, who had assisted North at the Treasury during an illness of John Robinson some years earlier and had then become one of the circle of subordinates in the minister's confidence. News of Saratoga led North to open an unofficial negotiation with the American Commissioners who were in Paris seeking French support, a move so sudden and secret that even Germain did not know of it beforehand. North's aim was an immediate peace that would preserve some link with America and avert the French war that was obviously imminent: but the result of his initiative was to allow Franklin and his colleagues to play off Britain against France. North soon realized that his idea had failed, and he began the preparation of proposals to put direct to Congress. During the Christmas recess he was deep in consultation not with his cabinet but with subordinates like Eden, Jenkinson and Solicitor-

---

* The political consequences of Saratoga are discussed in the next chapter.

General Wedderburn. By late January he reported to George III a draft scheme, comprising repeal of the tea duty and of the Massachusetts Government Act, and the dispatch to America of a Commission empowered to negotiate all outstanding points of dispute.[18] North completed his plans without consulting the cabinet beforehand: and he and Eden finally decided upon a complete renunciation of colonial taxation in theory and practice rather than repeal of specific legislation. North obtained reluctant cabinet approval of his proposals and presented them to the House of Commons on 17 February 1778, seeking parliamentary endorsement by a Taxation Act and an Act to authorize the appointment of a Conciliatory Commission.

North took the opportunity to review the whole American question, portraying himself as a moderate throughout the crisis. He had never proposed any colonial taxes, and it was therefore not inconsistent for him to put an end to them. When his 1774 legislation had not had the intended result he had put forward a conciliatory proposition 'before the sword was drawn', and he still believed that his 1775 proposal could be 'the most lasting bond of union between Great Britain and her colonies'. The Commission he now suggested would meet all colonial objections, since it was authorized to treat Congress 'as if it were a legal body' and empowered to order a cessation of fighting and the suspension of all laws. Mindful of the need not to appear to be surrendering to force and perhaps of his own earlier pledges on that point, North claimed that his own first reaction to the news of Saratoga had been to pursue the war with redoubled vigour: but on reflection he had thought it wiser to avoid further bloodshed and expenditure. The terms he now proposed, North declared, were the same as those he would seek at the moment of victory. The plan was approved without opposition: hard-liners were silenced by dismay, while Fox claimed that this was the Rockinghamite scheme proposed by Burke in 1775. The legislation passed with little discussion, though Wilkes voiced what must have been the doubts of many about North's sincerity, claiming that the peace plan was merely intended to shield the ministry from criticism in Britain.[19] That charge was untrue, for North was privately and vainly urging peace on the King, arguing that the cost even of victory would be financially disastrous: 'Great Britain will suffer more in the war than her enemies . . . not . . . by defeats, but by an enormous expense, which will ruin her, and will not in any degree be repaid by the most brilliant victories: Great Britain will undo herself while she thinks of punishing France.' The King never accepted this line of argument, and told North in 1779 that it was 'only weighing such events in the scale of a tradesman behind his counter'.[20]

North, having set on foot a mode of conciliation, then lost interest in the project: his lassitude led him to behave in a way that provided apparent justification for the opposition sneers that the scheme was a sham. He took little part in the final briefing of the Commission; and he allowed its slim chance of success to be further reduced both by restrictions on its discretionary powers introduced during the passage of the relevant legislation and by the choice of Commissioners. None of them enjoyed prestige or popularity in America. Head of the Commission was Gower's son-in-law, the inexperienced young Lord Carlisle: his two assistants were George Johnstone, a former Governor of West Florida, publicly opposed to colonial independence, and Eden, who had engineered his own choice for career reasons. The Carlisle Peace Commission was a fiasco. News of the American treaty with France preceded its arrival: and the colonists' determination to secure full independence can only have been strengthened by the simultaneous British withdrawal from Philadelphia.

The evacuation was part of the new strategy that resulted from Saratoga and the French intervention in the war. No further attempt would be made to reconquer New England, and Pennsylvania was given up. New York was retained as the chief British military base, with Sir Henry Clinton replacing Howe as Commander-in-Chief: but the British offensive was switched to the southern colonies. The counterpart of this more limited American strategy was an attack on the French West Indies, both to seek compensation for potential losses in America and as a pre-emptive strike before France could act in an area where attack was easier than defence. In this second and last phase of the war North still took little part in the formulation of strategy. He was busy with the financial and political consequences of the war, and excused himself on that ground from its conduct, as by implication in this letter of 2 March 1778 to Sandwich: 'I am at present engaged from morning to night with the House of Commons and the loan, but will attend any meeting where my presence is required.'[21]

There is little to tell of North's subsequent role in a war situation where Britain was increasingly over-matched as European foes made common cause with American rebels and where those responsible for the conduct of the war were inhibited from adopting bold measures. Germain and Sandwich were unpopular, and therefore made cautious by their political vulnerability. Britain fell back on a passive war policy, with North repeatedly declaring that the aim was to wear down her opponents: he told the House of Commons in 1781 that the avoidance of defeat might produce a just and honourable peace. For some years the steady advance of General Cornwallis through the southern colonies and the constant interchange of islands in the West Indies held out the promise of such a result. But the hope was frustrated by a combination of enemy enterprise and British misfortunes and mistakes that culminated in the surrender of Cornwallis at Yorktown in October 1781. When Germain told North the news, the Prime Minister opened his arms and said 'Oh God! It is all over!'[22]

6

PRIME MINISTER:
DECLINE AND FALL
1775–82

In the middle 1770s the political barometer appeared to be set fair for Lord North. He enjoyed the friendship as well as the confidence of his sovereign. He was the Leader of the House of Commons in more than name, commanding the loyalty of most M.P.s and the affection of all. Moreover, still only forty-three in 1775, he was entrenched in office for the foreseeable future. There was no credible rival within the administration, and the opposition factions were weakened, disheartened and divided. Especially did the Rockingham and Chatham groups differ in these years on the key question of America, with the former soon anxious to shed the colonial responsibility and the latter adamant to preserve the empire at all costs. There would be little parliamentary pressure to make the King dismiss his minister, and George III had long since made it clear that he would never willingly part with North.

After the experiences of his first decade as monarch George III thoroughly appreciated the advantage of having a minister with whom he enjoyed an easy personal relationship. North was charming and amusing, and at the same time modest and respectful, in closet and correspondence. He knew his duty to the throne, concerning the royal house as well as the government of the country: hence his determination to carry the unpopular Royal Family Marriage Act in 1772 even though he himself disliked the measure. George III in return always gave North any support he needed, in matters of patronage, in the handling of ministerial colleagues, and on issues of policy: and he characteristically reminded North of the fact from time to time, as in this letter of 1778:[1]

> From the hour of Lord North's so handsomely devoting himself on the retreat of the Duke of Grafton, I have never had a political thought which I have not communicated unto him, have accepted of persons highly disagreeable to me because he thought they would be of advantage to his conducting public affairs, and have yielded to measures my own opinion did not quite approve.

If North was not going to be removed by Crown or Parliament, would he leave office of his own accord? He certainly wanted the world to think that he was being kept on against his will by the King, and he did make frequent requests to be allowed to resign. But these were voiced in spells of depression, at times of parliamentary difficulty, and when there were awkward decisions to take; and they never led to any practical step on his part. He was like the man who is always threatening suicide and never commits it. North's whole career belies his claim that he was not ambitious for office. He was a politician to his fingertips, and what politician does not think that the power and prestige of being top man outweigh the disadvantages? North indeed accepted from George III obligations that he knew would make it morally impossible for him to resign against the King's wishes. The most notable instance was in September 1777, after John Robinson had told George III of North's financial difficulties. The King promptly offered to set North free of his personal debts: 'You know me very ill if you do not think that of all the letters I ever wrote to you this one gives me the most pleasure, and I want no other return but your being convinced that I love you as well as a man of worth as I esteem you as a Minister.' North gratefully accepted the offer, and by 1782 had received £16,062 from the royal purse.[2] In

1778 North put his finances on a sounder permanent basis by requesting and obtaining the place of Lord Warden of the Cinque Ports, receiving a salary of £1,000 when Prime Minister and a nominal £4,000 thereafter. These rewards had the political consequence that North felt himself unable to resign without the King's permission; and that he was never to obtain. The bond had become a chain.

Only Parliament would prise apart George III and Lord North, and that possibility seemed remote in 1775. In the House of Commons North's personal ascendancy had gradually been reinforced by a useful debating team, although he was to lose his two most effective legal mouthpieces there during the next few years. The formidable Attorney-General Thurlow went to the Lords in June 1778, replacing Bathurst, the former Apsley, as Lord Chancellor and becoming the strong man of the cabinet for the last years of the North ministry. The eloquent Solicitor-General Wedderburn, who succeeded Thurlow, followed him to the Upper House in June 1780 as Lord Loughborough. By then North was less dependent on them for parliamentary support than he had been earlier in the decade. In Germain he had acquired a cabinet colleague to share the burden of ministerial responsibility in the Commons. Other competent performers in the House were the well-informed Charles Jenkinson, who became Secretary at War in 1778, and Paymaster-General Richard Rigby, always good for a robust speech. Inevitably, too, the fact that North was firmly in the saddle attracted support both from the opposition, Charles Cornwall being the most notable acquisition, and from new M.P.s. Two important parliamentary recruits who entered the House at the general election of 1774 were William Eden and Henry Dundas, an able and forceful speaker who had Scottish offices heaped upon him: Lord Advocate of Scotland from 1775, he was to prove invaluable in debate during the closing years of the ministry.

The political barometer did not allow for the cloud of the American War: but although the conflict was to cause North's eventual resignation, it may also have had the paradoxical consequence of prolonging the life of his ministry. Certainly news of the outbreak of fighting in 1775 struck despair into the opposition. Rockingham, aware that the war had popular support both inside and outside Parliament, was not disposed to challenge North overmuch at Westminster: he rightly foresaw that the tide of political opinion would not turn without military setbacks abroad and economic distress at home. Above all he was concerned to prevent his faction from being branded the pro-American party: and in this he showed more wisdom than young Charles James Fox, who came to replace Dowdeswell, now deceased, as the Commons spokesman of his faction. The identification of the main parliamentary opposition group with the cause of American independence was to be an important factor in the longevity of the North administration. Not until the war was obviously lost would Parliament turn against the ministry. Good news from America was bad news for the opposition, who could make no capital at all out of the 1776 campaign, when Canada was recovered and New York captured. In the debate on the Address on 31 October 1776 North was therefore challenged primarily on the question of French naval rearmament. He told the House that the government had received pacific assurances from France, 'as strong as words can make them', but was nevertheless making ready some ships as a precaution. On the general question of the war North stated his intention of using the anticipated victory with 'prudence and moderation', and of allowing the colonists to tax themselves in future.[3] Administration won the division by 242 votes to 87, and there followed a Rockinghamite secession from Parliament for much of the session.

Even the news of Saratoga at the end of 1777 produced no immediate transformation of the political scene. The effect was felt at once in the cabinet, where North hoped for the resignation of Germain: that would allow a reconstruction of the ministry with the aim of ending the war.* This hope did not materialize, and the only cabinet change resulting from the disaster took place in March 1778, when Lord Amherst was given a seat on being appointed to the command of the army. Even though North secured the formal establishment of the Carlisle Peace Commission he was soon resigned to a continuation of the war: but he now began his attempts to shift responsibility for it to other shoulders. During March he vainly urged George III to invite Chatham to take over the administration before he made an alliance with the Rockingham party.[4] Chatham was in fact failing in health, and died the next month. His small group was soon led by Shelburne into the cooperation with Rockingham which North had feared, and by the autumn of 1778 the ministry was anticipating a difficult parliamentary session in view of two potential embarrassments: Admiral Keppel's failure to beat the French fleet off Ushant in July, and the emergence of an Irish problem.

For Saratoga had been the political watershed of the ministry, in

* For North's peace moves see above, pp. 108–10.

Parliament. Although opposition attacks early in 1778 were beaten off, the session saw a significant drop in the administration majority on America, from about 150 to 80 or 90. On 2 February 1778 an attempt by Fox to prevent more soldiers being sent to America was defeated by 259 votes to 165 without debate. Five days later a motion by Burke condemning the British use of Indians failed by 223 votes to 137: North's defence of their employment was that it was 'bad but unavoidable: that they were of that nature, that if one side did not, they would enter immediately on the other'.[5] The session had seen both a rise in the opposition vote and the abstention of administration supporters. North warned George III in November 1778 that this last problem might become worse:

> The strong measures that must be taken, the want of confidence and attachment to the present ministry, grounded on the bad success of their measures, together with some other circumstances, will, Lord North fears, render the Members of Parliament very indifferent to the cause of government, and much inclined to avoid doing their duty in Parliament.'[6]

But the political highlight of the ensuing winter did not take place at Westminster. It was the court martial of Keppel in Portsmouth. His acquittal in February 1779 was a triumph for the parliamentary opposition, which seized on the implication that the Admiralty had been at fault. On 3 March a Commons motion of censure on Sandwich was defeated by only thirty-four votes, 204 to 170, although North spoke 'with remarkable energy and confidence' and accepted cabinet responsibility for the decision to send out Keppel's fleet.[7]

North soon had more pressing worries on his mind than this ominous shift of parliamentary opinion. The death of Northern Secretary Suffolk the same month precipitated a crisis within the administration. North's intention was to bring Hillsborough back to the cabinet, but this was strongly opposed by Wedderburn and Eden, two ambitious men fishing in troubled waters. After Suffolk's demise they were the leaders of the old Grenvillite party, and contrived so to bully North by threats of resignation and demands for office that the appointment of a new Secretary of State was indefinitely postponed. The summer of 1779 saw North sunk in a slough of despond, taking no decisions on policies or appointments. George III, holding that 'if others will not be active, I must drive', summoned the cabinet himself on 21 June, a move by a sovereign unprecedented since Anne's reign. His aim was to give support to North, for the King knew that his Prime Minister was irreplaceable: he told Germain on 24 June that 'although he is not entirely to my mind, and there are many things about him I wish were changed, I don't know any who would do so well, and I have a great regard for him and very good opinion of him'.[8] Neither this royal initiative nor the incessant prodding of Robinson, Jenkinson and Eden had any effect. Their comments, and those of the King, have been extensively quoted by historians to document this low point of North's career as Prime Minister. Here is one sample, a letter from Robinson to Jenkinson on 11 August:[9]

> Nothing done, or attempting to be done; no attention to the necessary arrangements at home, none to Ireland, nothing to India . . . He is the most altered man I ever saw in my life. He has not spirits to set to anything. They are quite gone as to business, though well and full as to the table and amusements, and his judgement still good when you can fix his attention, but that is most difficult to do. He writes to me from Kent that 'nothing can be more miserable than I am' are his words.

It was Ireland that finally roused North. The change of British policy there in the previous decade had at first been successful in imposing more direct control: but the appointment of a resident viceroy polarized the political situation, providing Ireland with a visible symbol of her dependence on Britain. The American War precipitated an Irish crisis. The Irish Parliament voted approval of British policy, but the Patriot opposition, led now by Henry Grattan, expressed sympathy with the American cause, and Irishmen were to adopt similar patterns of resistance. The pro-American sentiment was stronger among Protestants than Catholics, many of whom enlisted in the British army; and there was never a danger of a Catholic rising even after France intervened openly in the contest. But the war brought economic depression to Ireland. It cut off the illegal trade to America and Europe, and the commercial restrictions long on the statute book began to hurt: they included a prohibition on direct Irish trade with the colonies, and a provision that wool and woollen goods could be exported only to Britain. There developed a demand for 'free trade', an abolition of restrictions so that Ireland would be on the same commercial basis as Britain.

North had known by early 1778 that he had an Irish problem on his hands, and one made more difficult in his opinion by the pusillanimous conduct of a new Lord-Lieutenant, the Earl of Buckinghamshire, whose appointment North had strongly opposed. From his arrival in Ireland in 1777 this viceroy displayed both a reluctance to discipline the Irish Parliament in the manner of his predecessors and a sympathy with Ireland's economic distress. Within a few months he was pressing North for commercial concessions; and in 1778 the subject was taken up by 'the Irish interest' in the British House of Commons. On 2 April Lord Nugent moved for a Committee on Irish trade, a proposal carried unanimously. When the Committee met on 7 April fears were expressed that British manufacturers would be undersold, but North strongly supported relaxation of the trade laws as a move that would ultimately benefit Britain as well as Ireland. Nugent was able to carry resolutions permitting Ireland to export anything to the colonies except wool and import anything except tobacco. Legislation was promptly introduced on these points, and the ministry was so closely associated with the policy that on 9 April one critic, Sir Cecil Wray, claimed that North had issued a *fiat* that the measure should pass that session and called on independent members to oppose it. There developed a vigorous campaign against the Irish proposals founded, according to Edmund Burke, on 'gross prejudice' and 'the selfish views of a few interested individuals'. During the next few weeks the fears of British manufacturers and merchants were reflected in a flood of over sixty petitions to the House of Commons. The objections were to Irish imports from the colonies, not to permission for Irish exports, and the bill for the latter purpose passed without difficulty; but the Irish Import Bill was strongly attacked on its second reading on 6 May. North spoke stoutly in its support, pointing out that even opponents of the measure agreed that something should be done for Ireland. Irish expectations had been raised, and he saw 'no reason why the present Bill should not pass'. He regarded it as only a first step, an earnest of an intention to help Ireland more substantially in the future. The second reading was carried by 126 votes to 77, but North for all his fine words changed his mind afterwards and allowed the bill to be killed by an adjournment motion on 25 May.[10]

The permission in 1778 to export to the colonies was regarded by the Irish lobby as a trifling concession, a token of ministerial goodwill but of little value without a corresponding right to import: ships would not cross the Atlantic empty one way. Events in Ireland now began to set the pace. When the Irish government failed to establish a militia authorized by legislation of 1778, voluntary military associations were created by leading Protestants: this Volunteer organization was 8,000 strong by May 1779 and eventually numbered about 20,000. It was against this background of an implicit military backing to Irish demands that the question of Irish trade came before the British Parliament in 1779. Nugent raised the subject on 19 January, saying that relief to the Irish economy would be to the interest of Britain herself; and several speakers warned the House not to lose Ireland as America had been lost. But hopes of further concessions to Ireland foundered on the hostility of British manufacturers that became evident in Parliament and outside. The difficulty was demonstrated on 10 March, when a motion merely for a Committee to consider permission for direct sugar imports into Ireland was carried by only five votes: and the parliamentary session ended without anything at all having been done. North had nevertheless shown his continued goodwill towards Ireland by instigating a motion on 26 May by one of his junior Treasury Lords that asked for statistics of Irish trade. It copied one already moved by Rockingham in the Lords, when Gower had rashly given a promise that something would be done for Ireland: and was accordingly denounced in the debate as a pretext for inaction. North's aim in fact was to contrive an opportunity for promising that he would obtain all possible information on the subject and for pointing out the difficulty of reconciling Irish and British interests.[11]

North sat on the fence not through indecision but because he was in a dilemma. He received no credit from the Irish lobby for the concessions of 1778, and was under pressure for more both from the Irish government under Buckinghamshire and from a parliamentary group that cut across the political alignment of administration and opposition. Moreover, it was now clear that both Rockingham and Shelburne intended to use the Irish situation as a political weapon against the ministry, even to the extent of worsening the problem: opposition debating comments on the potential menace of the Volunteers only served to stimulate recruiting in 1779. Yet the flood of petitions in 1778 and the statements of their spokesmen inside and outside Parliament made it clear that important British mercantile and manufacturing interests would oppose any further economic concessions to Ireland.

The problem was to be solved for North by events in Ireland, the establishment there of a boycott of British goods that silenced the opposition within Britain: for, in contrast to 1778, the Westminster Parliament did not receive a single petition in protest against the economic benefits North sought to bestow on Ireland at the end of 1779. The Irish non-importation agreements began in March 1779, and by May lists of offenders were being published in the Dublin press: in September Buckinghamshire informed the British government that adherence to the boycott had been much stricter than he could have imagined. It was this economic pressure rather than the better-known but more remote threat of the Volunteers that changed the political situation within Britain and made it possible for North to go ahead with the concessions he had already been contemplating when he was being denounced in Parliament for doing nothing. Even before the Commons debate of 26 May Buckinghamshire had been sent an official request for information on the economic state of Ireland. The viceroy sounded a wide range of Irish opinion, and the overall view was that 'free trade' would not cure all the ills of the Irish economy but would certainly alleviate the discontent. These conclusions had been sent to Southern Secretary Weymouth by mid-July: but although Ireland fell within his departmental responsibility he promptly passed the buck to North by forwarding them to the Treasury. There they remained for several months while nothing was done. The lethargy that afflicted North at this time was compounded on Ireland by resentment against his colleagues Gower and Weymouth for respectively making promises and evading responsibility, and by annoyance over the constant raising of Irish demands: he commented to Buckinghamshire on 30 July that his ministry had done more for Ireland in ten years than had been achieved during the rest of the century, a point that was a constant refrain of his parliamentary speeches.

All the emphasis of North's critics, past and present, on his personal failings misses the point. Those demanding action did not say what should or could be done about Ireland. It was not necessary for North to read more papers to grasp the problem. He was well aware of and sympathetic towards Irish economic grievances, and perturbed by the potential threat posed by the existence of the armed Volunteers: but during the summer of 1779 no solution to the Irish crisis was in sight. The trade boycott had not yet softened British hostility to further concessions.

The Irish question now ignited the ministerial problem North had hitherto shirked. Early in October Gower announced his resignation as Lord President of the Council, giving as the reason the administration's failure to do something for Ireland in fulfilment of his promise in the Lords. Gower was the leader of the old Bedford faction, and contemporaries suspected a plot to dislodge North by shattering what remained of his morale. North's response was not what might have been anticipated by his detractors: instead of flinching from the blow he appointed former diplomat Lord Stormont to fill the Northern Secretaryship left vacant for the last seven months. Speculation of a Bedfordite conspiracy was revived in November by the resignation of Weymouth as Southern Secretary. The key figure was now Lord Chancellor Thurlow. The general expectation was that the ministry would collapse if he followed his fellow-Bedfordites out of office. He did not do so, but North fell into a mood of despair and indecision, and even George III contemplated a coalition. He deputed Thurlow to make soundings for one, only for Thurlow to ascertain that no opposition leader would unite with North, Germain and Sandwich. By the end of November North had recovered his nerve. He decided to recall Bathurst to the cabinet as Lord President, and even to defy Wedderburn's objections by appointing Hillsborough as Southern Secretary.

The ministry survived almost despite itself. Germain and Sandwich were as politically vulnerable as ever, and the new ministers brought no accession of strength. North, who had discovered a correspondence of Robinson and George III behind his back, and resented the royal confidence recently given to Thurlow, continued to profess his desire to resign. Thurlow made no secret of his contempt for North's indecision: 'Damn him . . . Nothing can goad him forward. He is the very clog that loads everything.' But for him, as for such malcontents as Wedderburn, Eden and Rigby, North was the best Prime Minister they had. The patchwork ministry was to survive until final defeat in the American War.[12]

Already events during these very weeks of British political crisis had made possible a solution to the Irish question. The Irish trade boycott had by now undermined the hostility of English prejudice and vested interests at the same time as the decision of the Dublin Parliament to vote supplies for only six months and the menace of the Volunteers had brought home the danger of the Irish situation to opinion at Westminster. Realization that Irish discontent was developing into disorder came with news of a riot outside the Dublin Parliament on 15 November, and North now acted swiftly. When the Westminster Parliament met on 25 November assurances were given in both Houses that Ireland would receive economic concessions. Hillsborough informed the Lords that he had only accepted office on condition of Ireland having 'equal trade', and North told the Commons that Ireland was entitled to relief: 'England no doubt would grant her everything that could be given without injuring herself.'[13]

North moved his Irish proposals on 13 December. They comprised three motions, the first two being the repeal of existing prohibitions on the export from Ireland of wool and woollen goods and of glass. These were to form one bill and could be justified on grounds of equity: but the third proposition, to allow Ireland freedom of trade with the colonies, was portrayed by North as a generous concession.

E

Ireland had no claim to it, for the colonies had been created by Britain for her own benefit, North said, expounding the purest doctrines of mercantilism:

By every principle of justice, of the law of nations and the custom of the other powers of Europe who had settlements and distant dependencies, the mother country had an exclusive right to trade with, and to forbid all others from having any intercourse with them. Such an exclusive right was of the very essence of colonialism.

But it was in the interest of Britain to promote the commerce of Ireland, and this was the only prudent way to do so, one that would convince Ireland of British goodwill and put an end to the discontent there. North ended with an appeal for consideration of the subject without 'local prejudices and national partialities'. The opposition, uncertain of the reception of the plan in Ireland, greeted it without either enthusiasm or criticism. Only Charles James Fox spoke, to say that their silence implied acquiescence rather than approval: the resolutions were solely the responsibility of the administration, not the result of parliamentary consideration. The opposition emerged from the Irish crisis with little credit: mischievous incitement of Irish resistance was followed by failure to welcome a realistic solution of the problem. The first Irish Bill passed the same month, and after the Christmas recess North introduced the one to allow Ireland to trade with the colonies: by the end of February 1780 it had also become law with little debate.[14]

North was very anxious about the reception of his policy in Ireland. A hostile reaction there would leave him worse off than before, facing an angry Britain as well as a discontented Ireland. He need not have worried. The Irish Parliament displayed gratitude in debates and resolutions, bestowing generous praise on both Buckinghamshire and North. It was accompanied by Irish criticism of Fox and his friends for not having welcomed the proposals: on 21 December 1779 the viceroy informed Germain that 'the triumph of Lord North and the disgrace of his English opponents were equally complete'.[15]

By early 1780 the North ministry had solved an Irish crisis that had threatened to develop into another American situation. Within the British government satisfaction was tempered by the demand for a scapegoat, the dismissal of the Lord-Lieutenant on the ground that the whole problem had been due to his political mismanagement. North resisted the pressure for his recall, being well aware that this superficial judgement on a complex situation did scant justice to the viceroy and fearing that such a step would merely exacerbate a

situation that had not returned to normal. The delay in meeting the
economic grievances had sown the seeds of future trouble, for the
protracted nature of the crisis had generated a political consciousness
in Ireland that found continuing expression in resentment at the
subordination of the Dublin Parliament to British control. By
March 1780 eighteen counties had petitioned for repeal of Poyning's
Law. The North ministry decided to countenance no constitutional
changes at all, and sent instructions to Dublin in good time. In April
the Irish government beat off a Patriot attack in Parliament,
defeating a repeal motion and also a resolution by Grattan that only
the Dublin Parliament could legislate for Ireland. The Irish constitutional grievance continued to smoulder, but did not blow up
into a flame until near the end of North's ministry. It was on 15
February 1782 that a representative meeting of the Ulster Volunteers
at Dungannon called for Irish legislative independence. North
resigned while this demand was being copied all over Ireland, and
the issue was bequeathed to his successors.

With the Irish problem temporarily resolved, and the war campaigns seemingly successful, the parliamentary challenge North
faced in 1780 was on the question of political reform at home.
Towards the end of 1779 widespread concern over government
extravagance and corruption was given coherent expression by a
Yorkshire landowner, Christopher Wyvill. Under his leadership
there sprang up in the space of a few months a national agitation on
the subject of 'Economical Reform', with the aim of reducing
government expenditure by the abolition of sinecures, pensions, and
other traditional methods of political influence. That was the central
theme of the so-called Yorkshire Movement, although alteration of
the electoral system by 'Parliamentary Reform' and even the creation of a National Convention of delegates as an anti-Parliament
were the objectives of some reformers. In the first months of
1780 dozens of petitions poured in to the House of Commons
from counties and boroughs. Although spontaneous in origin, a
grass-roots reaction from provincial England, this movement
was encouraged by the parliamentary opposition, and the North
administration was threatened with defeat on a popular issue over
which it seemed particularly vulnerable.[16]

It was an opportunity for North to deploy his political skills. In
the debates over the petitions and an Establishment Bill introduced
by Edmund Burke to abolish certain specified offices North adopted
in succession two alternative tactics. He sought first to blunt the
opposition weapon by repeatedly pointing out that the petitions

represented the views not of whole counties or boroughs but only of those persons who had signed them, and they, he claimed, were always a minority of the electorate. This was a dangerous game to play. When on 23 February North denied that the petitions were 'the voice of the people of England, Yorkshire M.P. Sir George Savile tartly rejoined that North had said the same about petitions from America and ought to learn from experience. The direct challenge on economical reform North sought to sidestep by welcoming the idea in principle, as when on 14 February he declared that no M.P. could favour economy more than he did. He suggested a permanent Committee of Accounts, and stole much of the opposition thunder by announcing on 2 March the creation of the Commission of Accounts that was to produce so much valuable evidence in the next few years.* The tactic of welcoming the reforming ideas in principle while objecting to all proposals was a political tightrope to walk, and North was so conscious of this that he underwent the rare experience for him of losing his temper in debate when opposition members laughed at him on 21 February. It was nevertheless a tightrope to success, as the battle over Burke's bill was fought out on individual clauses in Committee. Except for an irrelevant altercation with the Speaker, North did not speak in the three main debates: on 8 March, when the American Secretaryship was saved by 208 votes to 201; on 13 March, when the opposition carried the abolition of the Board of Trade by 207 votes to 199; and on 20 March, when an attack on offices in the Royal Household was beaten off by 211 votes to 158.[17]

Then came the famous motion by John Dunning on 6 April that 'the influence of the Crown has increased, is increasing, and ought to be diminished'. This was a basic question of principle such as North had been disposed to concede. He rose late in the debate, goaded into speech by opposition comments on his silence, and put the best face he could on the situation. He condemned the motion as an abstract proposition, contrary to parliamentary rules, and heatedly accused his opponents of 'pursuing measures likely to overthrow the constitution'. Called to order he avowed his words and rashly asked, 'Am I to hear myself charged as the author of our present misfortunes?', to be met with loud opposition cries of 'You are! You are!'. North resumed his speech only after considerable confusion in the House, and then claimed that the behaviour of the opposition kept him in office because 'the people at large considered them as dangerous to their liberties'. Altogether it was a poor performance

* See above, pp. 105–6.

by North, unconvincing alike in his rejoinder that Parliament itself was responsible for American policy and in his argument that so many reform measures were already before the House that further steps would be improper and unnecessary. The imminence of defeat had rattled North. Dunning's motion was carried by 233 votes to 215, and Burke jibed that a minister in a minority was 'a curiosity . . . more fit for the British Museum than the British House of Commons'.[18]

North promptly told the King that he wanted to resign at the end of the session: George III ruefully replied that the resolution had been aimed at him, not his minister.[19] It soon became clear that the House of Commons had no desire to see North replaced by his opponents. This attitude represented more than a simple preference for North over Fox, although that alone was a strong enough motive for many independent M.P.s. By 1780 the opposition had become identified with a policy of conceding American independence to gain peace, and that was a step still unacceptable to most members. A number of them, having made a gesture on Dunning's motion, wanted to take matters no further, and the next few weeks saw the defeat of all the economic reform measures. After an administration majority of 254 to 203 on 24 April an angry Fox called it a disgraceful result, berating the members who had gone back on their votes of 6 April. North seized the chance of comparing this petulance with his own behaviour on that occasion: he had not then accused 'those who had frequently before voted with him, with baseness, treachery . . . and other improper motives'.[20] North was again master of the House.

But the shocks of the session had already led to ministerial thinking about a snap general election, and events during the summer converted this into a firm plan. The anti-Catholic Gordon riots that erupted in London during June showed the ministry in a bad light, paralysed by indecision and slow to use troops, although North displayed personal courage both in a street attack on him and when a crowd threatened 10 Downing Street on 7 June: yet the administration reaped the political dividend of being the bastion of order against 'the mob'. In an atmosphere of a common cause of men of property North approached Rockingham on 28 June with the offer of a coalition. Circumstances seemed propitious for the move. A breach had been developing between the two opposition factions over the reform movement, with Rockinghamites concerned only for Economical Reform and Shelburnites anxious for Parliamentary Reform as well; and while the Rockingham party had been cooperative over riot suppression the Shelburne group had been critical and even obstructive. The invitation to Rockingham was part of North's overall political strategy of seeking wider support, not an alternative to a general election, which North formally suggested to the cabinet on 1 July. Rockingham's terms for an alliance proved to be too high: he demanded royal permission for American independence, parliamentary enactment of the economical reform programme, and cabinet changes involving the dismissal of Sandwich and Germain and the replacement of Hillsborough and Stormont by Fox and Richmond. The negotiations ended abruptly, for these proposals were quite unacceptable not only to the King but to North and his colleagues, men made increasingly optimistic about their political prospects by the news in June of the capture of Charleston in South Carolina and by John Robinson's analysis of the current state of patronage and influence; there is a story that a friend called to sound North on the subject of the election at the very time Treasury Secretaries Robinson and Cooper were examining their lists and that North made this reply: 'I really cannot say more than this, that the doctors are now met in consultation on the case in the other room, and you know the result on such occasions is generally death.'[21] The ministerial calculation was that government action could gain twenty or thirty seats. North made little allowance for the possible impact of public opinion, although he did postpone any announcement for some weeks in case of bad war news. There followed a deliberate deception of the opposition leaders by North's ostentatious departure from London and his secret return: the dissolution of Parliament on 1 September caught the opposition unprepared.[22]

The success of the ministry's tactics failed to produce the gains anticipated. Holding the election did enable the administration to remove a few members sitting for government constituencies who had deserted to the opposition, and to improve its position in the small rotten and pocket boroughs: North took the usual Treasury role in negotiations with patrons and candidates, and the government expenditure of over £50,000 was a record. But Robinson's forecasts were ruined by losses in popular constituencies, the counties and larger boroughs, even though political issues such as the American War played hardly any more part than usual. The overall result appears to have been a net ministerial loss of some six seats.[23]

The outcome sowed uncertainty in the minds of both administration and opposition. North was uneasy about the task of carrying government business in the Commons, Rockingham pessimistic over the prospects of any attack save on Economical Reform. Certainly

the course of the war seemed to rule out America as a subject of
debate after the ministry triumphed on the Address by 212 votes to
130 on 6 November. Battle was not joined in earnest until early in
1781, when on 15 February Burke reintroduced his Establishment
Bill of the previous year. An analysis of the Commons by Robinson
the day before forecast a single-figure ministerial lead. Such a tiny
majority would start a wave of desertions, and a defeat might conceivably occur. North did not risk a vote then, but no minister
could remain long in such a humiliating position. On 26 February
North took the plunge, and defeated the bill on the second reading
by 233 votes to 190 even though he did not speak himself in the
debate. This was the turning-point of the session. North's depression
evaporated, and he had little difficulty in the Commons thereafter.
The House would not dismiss him over such an issue. The fate of his
administration depended on the war.[24]

The session of 1781 saw not only North's political survival but also
his postponement of any further settlement of the Indian problem.
After the legislation of 1773 the plan of the North ministry had been
to control the London end of the East India Company and to leave
the Indian territories to the rule of the new Governor-General,
Warren Hastings, and his Council. The task at India House fell to
John Robinson, under the general supervision of North. It was
attempted not by the purchase of stock but through parliamentary-
type management, the creation of 'a government interest' of M.P.s,
officials and other supporters who were already proprietors. This
method never provided more than a sure vote of about 30 per cent
in the General Court of Proprietors, and proved a failure in the most
significant trial of strength, when an attempt by the ministry to
recall Hastings was overruled there in 1776. The North administration continued for some years to support Philip Francis and other
critics of Hastings, but decided to retain the Governor-General when
the French entry into the war posed a threat in India; and in 1780,
for reasons of internal Company politics, North made an alliance with
the Hastings faction in India House under Laurence Sulivan. His
ministry's attitude towards Hastings was to be an embarrassment
to North when the conduct of Hastings became a burning political
issue in the middle 1780s.

The ministerial motive for interference in the East India Company
was to ensure good government in India and not, as some contemporaries suspected, to obtain patronage. The long-term aim was to
improve the stop-gap solution devised in 1773 when the Company's
charter was renewed in 1780. During the 1770s the ministry acquired

a very detailed knowledge of the Company's problems both in India and at home, and by 1778 Robinson had drafted plans that would secure greater government control over the Company and obtain more of its money for the state. They were submitted to North in November of that year, but Robinson could not prevail on him to act. The political situation was less favourable for government intervention than in 1773, for now a recalcitrant Company would be championed by a strong parliamentary opposition. On 21 March 1780 North responded to unacceptable proposals from India House by a Commons resolution threatening to end the Company's charter, and an angry debate ensued. Fox asked if North was not content with having lost America: did he now intend to destroy Britain's position in India?[25] The parliamentary situation in 1780 caused the postponement of Indian legislation until 1781, when it transpired that the mountain of labour by Robinson, Jenkinson and their associates had produced a mouse. The Company's charter was renewed for ten years, without any significant alteration either of its constitution or of the mode of government in India. Moreover, the state received no immediate financial return for granting the privilege, merely a claim to participate in the Company's profits. Contemporaries blamed North himself for the government's failure to take effective action. Sulivan, who had compared him for boldness with Oliver Cromwell eight years earlier, now complained of 'the timidity of Lord North'. He was not the minister he had been.[26]

A year later he was not minister at all. The American campaigns seemed to be going well in 1780 and 1781, with the successful advance of General Cornwallis through the southern colonies: and although some concern had been voiced about his situation in Virginia, no such disaster as Yorktown had been remotely expected. In the autumn of 1781 North was anticipating a quiet session when Parliament met on 27 November, and the opposition leaders were making little effort to muster their friends at Westminster. The news on 25 November of Cornwallis's defeat and surrender was so unforeseen that the administration had a brief respite before the parliamentary storm broke. The majority for approving the Address two days later, 218 votes to 129, was virtually identical with that of the year before. Nor had North himself reflected on the implications of Yorktown, for he said in the debate that the object of the war was still to 'procure a peace consistent with the legislative powers over the Colonies'.[27]

Whether this statement was bluff or unthinking bravado, North had changed his mind within a fortnight and come round to the necessity of conceding independence: but he knew that a public statement to that effect would both be against the national interest and bring down the ministry. News of such an admission in America would have a demoralizing effect on the conduct of the rest of the war and be a disastrous start to any peace negotiations. At home it would shatter the ministerial majority, uneasily divided between those who, like Germain, still wanted to retain sovereignty over America and those who wished to continue the war only against France and Spain. When on 12 December the opposition at last staged a major debate on America, North therefore resorted to a formula which would cover both points of view. He declared that 'it would not be wise nor right to go on with the American War as we had done'.[28] Possibly only this deliberately vague statement saved the ministry from defeat: that was the opinion of some M.P.s after the opposition attack was beaten off by 220 votes to 179. Two days later, when Germain was advocating the continuation of the American War, North deliberately rose from the Treasury Bench and found another seat behind, 'mute eloquence', as diarist Wraxall commented, to the disagreement he could not publicly avow.[29]

Beyond such gestures as this unique parliamentary charade North could not go. He had not obtained the consent of his sovereign to a change of policy, and was never to do so. George III was even more determined to continue the American War than Germain. When in the second half of December North raised the question of independence with the King, George III made it clear in both conversation and correspondence that he would not concede it.[30] This left North in an impossible position. The verbal compromise in the debate of 12 December had won a respite, but the House of Commons no longer contained a majority for continuation of the American War. There was to follow the irony of North's resignation over a policy that he had abandoned but from which he could not openly disassociate himself.[31]

Within the ranks of the ministry there were those who sought to avert the political consequence of military defeat. In December and January North came under heavy pressure to drop Germain and Sandwich from Lord Advocate of Scotland Henry Dundas, aided and abetted by Paymaster-General Richard Rigby. Dundas, a forceful and able debater and leader of a band of Scottish M.P.s, had hitherto been a strong partisan of the war. He now faced up to the reality that America was lost. His aim was to save the ministry by removing its chief political liabilities: Germain was the symbol of the war, and naval humiliations had made Sandwich vulnerable. North resisted

the demand. He knew Sandwich to be a very competent departmental minister, while he saw no political advantage in being rid of
Germain so long as the King vetoed independence and wanted to
retain him as a Commons spokesman.[32] His hand was forced when on
22 January Dundas and Rigby announced that they would not
attend Parliament until Germain was removed. Such a step would
destroy North's precarious majority, and Germain was replaced by
a stop-gap administrator, Welbore Ellis. But the delay over the
change, and George III's continued refusal to allow any alteration of
policy, made the jettisoning of Germain a futile expedient. The last
act of North's ministry was now to be played out, on the appropriate
stage of the House of Commons.[33]

The battle between administration and opposition in February
and March 1782 is one of the high points of parliamentary history:
the Commons forced the resignation of a minister the King wished to
retain. It began with a morale-shattering blow to North on 7
February, when a motion by Fox on naval mismanagement was
defeated only by twenty-two votes, 205 to 183. Both sides mustered
their forces when Fox tried again on 20 February, to lose by nine-
teen votes in a House of 458 members. The opposition, encouraged
by abstentions and desertions among administration supporters,
then turned to the issue of the war itself. North was here in the
infuriating position of being attacked for a policy, continuation of
the war with America, that he had given up but could not disclaim.
Taunted by Barré on 22 February he lost his temper and denounced
his adversary as 'insolent and brutal', language more temperate
than Barré's, but for which he at once apologized.[34] Feelings were
running high that day as the ministry defeated a motion by Conway
to end the American War by only one vote. Five days later Conway
put forward another, to stop 'offensive war' in America. North,
reminding M.P.s that he was speaking not to the House alone but to
'all the world', was unable to agree in public that America had been
lost. All he could do was ask for a vote of confidence, but this last
card failed. The attraction of Conway's motion to independent M.P.s
was such that it was carried by 234 votes to 215. About thirty of the
forty-odd of his habitual supporters who abstained or deserted
North in this division on 27 February intended only to force an end
to the war, not his resignation. They would prefer North to negotiate
a peace rather than his opponents, and the hope that George III
would now change his mind and allow North to do so kept the
ministry from resigning. But even after this parliamentary vote the
most George III would concede was a settlement based on 'keeping

what is in our present possession in North America'.[35] The North ministry was broken by parliamentary hammer-blows on the anvil of the King's unrealistic and unreasoning obstinacy over America.[36]

After the debate of 27 February North obtained the King's permission to strengthen his parliamentary position by negotiating a coalition: but attempts to ally with such politicians as Grafton and Shelburne proved unsuccessful, and no approach was made to the main opposition party under Rockingham.[37] North soon came round to the view that the defeat of 27 February had not been a vote of no confidence, and announced in the Commons that he would continue as minister until dismissed by the King or forced to resign by 'the sense of the House'. He still had a majority in the Commons, for some of those who had deserted him on 27 February returned to the ministerial fold: but that vote had in reality sealed his fate. Now that the American question had been settled, the administration began to lose the support of those other M.P.s who had long distrusted its capacity but had supported it for its resolute stand against conceding American independence.

The administration's war record made it ever vulnerable, a weakness emphasized by the news early in March of the loss of Minorca. The opposition tactics of undermining confidence in the ministry comprised a great deal of parliamentary sniping, but only two major trials of strength proved necessary. On 8 March a motion calling for the immediate removal of the ministry was defeated by ten votes, 226 to 216. There followed an approach by North to Rockingham, which led to a demand for a complete change of administration and strengthened opposition confidence in the outcome of the parliamentary contest. Robinson was meanwhile making a frantic effort to rally administration supporters for the next clash, a motion of no confidence on 15 March. He anticipated a majority of twenty or even thirty, but the ministry obtained one of only nine votes, 236 to 227. During the next few days realization dawned that this division had been decisive: and a deadline for dignified resignation had been fixed by the announcement of an opposition motion for 20 March calling for the removal of the ministry. Still George III refused to allow North to go, and a constitutional deadlock loomed ahead. On 18 March a group of independent M.P.s informed North that they were withdrawing their support from him, being 'of opinion that vain and ineffectual struggles tend only to public mischief and confusion'. North at once told the King that this step would put him in a minority, and set out the constitutional position in a famous letter that has become a significant document of modern British history:[38]

> Your Majesty has graciously and steadily supported the servants you approve, as long as they could be supported. Your Majesty has firmly and resolutely maintained what appeared to you essential to the welfare and dignity of this country, as long as the country itself thought proper to maintain it. The Parliament have altered their sentiments, and as their sentiments whether just or erroneous must ultimately prevail, Your Majesty having persevered, as long as possible, in what you thought right, can lose no honour if you yield at length, as some of the most renowned and most glorious of your predecessors have done, to the opinion and wishes of the House of Commons.

George III refused to discuss the subject with North until shortly before the Commons met on 20 March, and then accepted the resignation with the utmost reluctance after an interview of over an hour. Horace Walpole heard that 'the King parted with him rudely without thanking him, adding "Remember, my Lord, that it is you who desert me, not I you"'.[39] Noisy scenes erupted in the Commons before the opposition permitted North to announce the end of his administration. Nothing became North so well as his manner of quitting office. Wraxall remembered his 'equanimity, suavity and dignity' as he thanked the House for its long and steady support, which he would always deem 'the chief honour of his life', and declared his readiness to answer at any time for 'his public conduct'. The only member to have a carriage ready by the door at the unexpectedly early end to the parliamentary sitting, North left with a cheerful quip to the throng of M.P.s waiting outside on a bleak evening for their own coaches: 'Good night, gentlemen, you see what it is to be in the secret.' William Adam was one of the M.P.s invited by North to have the credit of dining with 'a fallen minister on the day of his dismissal', and always remembered the happy family atmosphere of the North household that evening.[40] It was a day of relief rather than regret for North.

7

FINAL DECADE:
COALITION
AND OPPOSITION
1782–92

North's resignation did not imply his retirement from politics.[1] Still only forty-nine years of age, he took out of office with him a large parliamentary following, over a hundred strong in the Commons. This personal support was partly the result of his long years of patronage; partly a testimony to his ability and character; and partly due to calculation about his future political prospects as an excellent parliamentarian and capable administrator still high in favour with his sovereign. Many must have envisaged another North ministry, and that might indeed have occurred if George III had not found a new political saviour in young William Pitt.

It was not long before North's political future began to look brighter. The second Rockingham ministry that took office on his fall had a short and troubled life. It was an enforced alliance between the two former opposition factions: the parliamentary strength of the Rockingham group obliged the King to accept them as the basis of his new administration, even though George III would have preferred to have Shelburne as his Prime Minister. Within this coalition there was constant bickering over patronage and argument over policy: in particular Shelburne was still reluctant to concede America the independence that the Rockinghamites had long deemed to be inevitable.

This ministerial discord soon brought North back into the political reckoning without any move on his part. During the early weeks of the new administration the Northites lay low, sunk in pessimism and cowed by wild talk of impeachment. They put up little resistance to the Economical Reform programme now at last enacted by their opponents. But North's party held the parliamentary balance of power when the ministry fell apart in July. The death of Rockingham on 1 July merely precipitated a crisis stemming from the distrust felt for Shelburne by Charles James Fox, Rockingham's political heir. When the King at once asked Shelburne to be the new Prime Minister, Fox, aware that he himself was personally unacceptable to his sovereign, put forward the Duke of Portland as the choice of the cabinet. On George III's rejection of this demand Fox resigned and took with him into opposition the bulk of the old Rockinghamite party. That month saw the Northites courted by both factions. Shelburne secured the allegiance of Henry Dundas, with North's blessing, and the support of Jenkinson and Robinson: but other friends of North like Eden and Loughborough were urging him towards an alliance with Fox.

North's attitude was complicated by a sharp deterieration in his friendship with the King. At his resignation he had informed George III that a large debt still remained on the 1780 election account, £30,000 borrowed from the King's banker Henry Drummond on George III's authority and £2,754 owed to North personally; but on 18 April the King accepted responsibility for only £13,000 and unfairly threw on North the burden of a public debt equal to several years of his personal income. North accepted this decision without protest on 18 May: 'Lord North, having no money, and not being able to give Mr Drummond any security, is endeavouring to arrange his affairs in such a manner as to be able to apply the whole income of his office*

* Warden of the Cinque Ports.

to the gradual extinction of the debt.'[2] The effect of George III's behaviour was to outweigh his earlier financial generosity to North: the King had left his former minister with a debt of £17,000 and an interest charge of over £2,000, and he had also ignored North's claim to the £2,754 spent out of his own money.[3] Yet George III apparently could not conceive of the possibility that this treatment might have made North disenchanted with his sovereign; for on 7 August the King asked him to support the Shelburne ministry in language recalling their old relationship: 'Lord North has so often whilst in office assured me that whenever I could consent to his retiring he would give the most cordial support to such an administration as I might approve of.' North sent a cool and non-committal reply.[4]

North was in high spirits by late summer, Edward Gibbon noting in September that he looked 'not so fat and more cheerful than ever'.[5] His customary good humour was doubtless increased by the novel freedom from the strain of office and by the competition for his favour. Never the man to make decisions in a hurry, North refrained from promising support to either side. His normal inclination to back the King's government was balanced by his personal feelings; he thought George III had been unfair to him in the matter of the debt, while he disliked Shelburne and distrusted his reforming notions. Ministerial confidence of his eventual support overestimated his loyalty to the King and took no account of two other factors: the pressure of North's followers for some move that would restore them to office and his own reaction to the peace settlement Shelburne concluded with the American colonies in November; it failed to provide adequate safeguards for the Loyalists, a subject on which North was naturally sensitive.

No one knew what would happen when Parliament re-assembled at the end of the year, but all the political guessing-games under-lined the significance of North's position: the best-known calculation, made by William Eden in October, gave Shelburne 140 followers, North 120 and Fox 90, with some 200 M.P.s undecided. When the session opened North had still made no decision, and informed his followers that he was connected with neither administration nor opposition. He dominated the first debate of 5 December on the Address, criticizing Fox for demanding prompt and unconditional recognition of American independence, warning the Shelburne ministry not to abandon the Loyalists, and claiming for his own administration the credit for Rodney's great naval victory at the Battle of the Saints.[6] That North's debating skill was backed by voting power was shown when Fox tested the Commons by forcing a division on 18 December. The Northites secured a crushing majority for the administration of 219 votes to 46, but only after North had made a witty speech critical of the ministry;[7] and Edmund Burke made this comment on the political situation at the end of 1782:[8]

If it were in my Lord North's power to command our conduct whenever he thought proper to come, and that we could not move but at his pleasure, we could never consider ourselves as an independent party . . . Nothing could be so disgraceful to the gentlemen who act as ministers as the victory obtained for them by Lord North. They looked . . . more like captives led before the conqueror than parties in the triumph.

North held the balance of power when Parliament adjourned for the Christmas recess: but he would have to decide what to do when the peace terms came before Parliament for ratification in February, and the competition for his alliance grew hotter in 1783. Shelburne's failure to grasp the danger of the parliamentary situation made him slow to act; and he was handicapped by the implacable hostility felt towards North by his twenty-three-year-old Leader of the House, William Pitt. Too young to know the story at first hand, and brought up on a diet of opposition propaganda, Pitt regarded North as the man responsible for the American War and as a minister whose administration had been the embodiment of unconstitutional influence. His antipathy had been intensified by his role as the chief target of North's raillery during the debates of December.[9] Henceforth the dominant fact in North's political life was to be the vendetta conducted against him by Pitt, who embarked on an incessant personal onslaught on North during the Commons debates of the next few years.[10] Political calculation may well have reinforced Pitt's motivation; for with Fox ruled out by royal hatred, North in the 1780s was the only M.P. who could conceivably be an alternative minister to Pitt, and so the last shreds of his reputation had to be destroyed.

Pitt's veto precluded any direct offer by Shelburne to North, who came to suspect the ministerial soundings as a trick: he would be left holding a bundle of vague promises once the peace terms had been carried by his voting strength. Within North's own party a fierce contest for his ear was being waged. If Robinson told North that having lost the war himself he could not honourably oppose the resultant peace terms, Eden argued that North could not possibly approve them. Dundas tried to panic North into supporting the peace by conjecturing that the resignation of Shelburne would lead to a Fox–Pitt coalition, with North in the political wilderness: but this tactic misfired.[11] North promptly sent his son George to arrange a meeting with Fox. This took place on 13 February, and during the next few days the problems of forming a coalition were ironed out before the parliamentary debates on the peace. The two men agreed on an alliance in principle, postponing decisions on the spoils of office until after the moment of victory. On policy they found little difficulty. The American War and Economical Reform were now dead issues, and they were able to reconcile their attitudes on the two other points of difference. Parliamentary Reform, favoured by Fox and opposed by North, was to be left an open question; while on the subject of the Loyalists North was to move a separate resolution condemning their alleged betrayal. More important than such details was the agreement of the two men on the basic constitutional issue. North had always regarded Parliament as being more important than the Crown. He had made this clear to George III on his resignation in the previous March, and Fox could have found no fault with the constitutional doctrine North now expounded to him: 'The King ought to be treated with all sort of respect and attention, but the appearance of power is all that a King of this country can have.'[12] That George III did not accept this interpretation and was to give a practical demonstration of its inadequacy during the next year does not invalidate the point that North's role in the constitutional crisis of 1783–4 was entirely consistent with his earlier career.

In his public defence of the coalition North employed the argument of national interest; he told the Commons on 21 February: 'There are certainly times and circumstances and emergencies, when it highly becomes all honest men, of every party and description, manfully to relinquish their personal feuds and temporary animosities, and unite their serious efforts by one generous exertion, in their common interest.'[13] He was claiming to be practising what the King had always preached about party, but George III saw the matter in quite a different light! Ignoring the political issues and pressures of the time, the King both then and later regarded North's action as a 'desertion' of the throne in its hour of need.[14]

North led the attack in the Commons debate on the peace that began on 17 February and lasted through the night until after dawn the next day. He argued that the ministry should not have presumed to seek parliamentary approval of such a peace: there was a precedent to the contrary, Henry Pelham in 1748 having merely laid the unsatisfactory terms of the Peace of Aix-la-Chapelle before the House for information. The question, North said, was not whether he himself could have done better, but 'whether this is such a peace as ought to have been made' at all. He then criticized in particular the concessions to France, the generous treatment of America and the desertion of the Loyalists.[15] The coalition proved a parliamentary success, for the debate ended in an opposition majority of 224 votes to 208. The two factions had stood firm in the face of misgivings about the coalition, North polling some 117 followers and Fox about 72: but the ministry had obtained the support of most independent members, and the narrow margin encouraged Shelburne to stand a second trial on 21 February. A masterly speech by Pitt, blaming the peace terms on North's mismanagement of the war and attacking the 'unnatural coalition', failed to avert a second defeat, by 207 votes to 190, and Shelburne tendered his resignation on 24 February.[16]

Pitt's denunciation of the coalition as unprincipled was to be echoed by many contemporaries and later by a number of historians, to the detriment of North's reputation as well as more conspicuously that of Fox. Such abuse was hypocritical, or naïve. Acute observers had been aware since July 1782 that only some coalition could resolve the political situation. Since Fox refused to ally with Shelburne, and Pitt forbade Shelburne to do so with North, a Fox–North coalition was the logical outcome, and one more offensive to political innocents than to realists. Both men had respect for each other's integrity, and neither sacrificed principles in making their alliance. Historical judgements should not be based on the indignation of an angry George III or the malign slanders of a thwarted Pitt, men whose own behaviour at the end of 1783 was to be of far more dubious constitutional propriety. The coalition was a mature approach to politics, but unfortunately for Fox and North it was one too sophisticated for contemporary opinion.

Pitt was asked to lead a new ministry, hesitated, and refused by the end of the month. George III predictably then sought to detach North from Fox. On 2 March the King sent through Guilford an 'offer of placing him again in the Treasury and consulting him on the formation of a ministry on the most comprehensive lines'. If this plan was unacceptable to North he could still have a cabinet office and be consulted on the formation of a ministry under a peer 'not connected with any of the strong parties'. North's reply, delivered through his father next day, comprised a refusal of any office but a willingness to be consulted by the King. George III saw him at nine o'clock that evening, and offered the coalition office under 'an independent peer'. This stipulation proved the stumbling-block. Fox would not accept the device of a ministry under a royal nominee, and replied the next day that he and his friends would serve only under the Duke of Portland. George III interviewed North at nine o'clock again that evening, asking him whether a ministry could be formed between his friends and the remnant of the Shelburne administration. North tactfully gave no immediate answer, but on the following day, 5 March, wrote to say that the plan was impossible.[17]

George III surrendered to the coalition after a week spent desperately and vainly looking for any alternative ministry. On 12 March he told North that he would accept Portland at the Treasury. Negotiations about the new administration then continued for the rest of the month, as the two parties to the coalition sought to agree on a distribution of offices and rejected the King's demand for a full list of appointments beforehand. George III took the opportunity to make another approach to Pitt, who finally declined to risk an administration after the Coalition had demonstrated its parliamentary power in a Commons debate of 24 March; for as minister he would have been entirely dependent on North's goodwill. George III had to capitulate to whatever the coalition demanded, and on 1 April sent for North to announce that he would accept Portland's cabinet list without further details of the new administration. Privately, however, the King made known his intention of dismissing the coalition as soon as possible; and publicly he signified his disapproval by a determination to show no favours to the ministers, notably by his refusal to create any peerages at their request.

This regal behaviour not only advertised George III's dislike of his new ministers; it also upset their planning, such as the idea that North should go to the House of Lords to strengthen their debating-team there. Instead he resumed a seat on the Treasury Bench, now Home Secretary to Fox's Foreign Secretary, with son George as his Under-Secretary. North had proved very cooperative in the detailed formation of the ministry. Despite their numerical superiority the Northites took only three of the seven cabinet places, and no more than a slight majority of the lesser posts. That this administration was one of considerable talent was doubted by few contemporaries: but the enmity of the King put it in the same position as a present-day ministry confronted by a hostile electorate. Unless there was a change of heart, a day of reckoning would come; and George III was to prove less fickle than twentieth-century public opinion. Meanwhile the country had to be governed: a loan was raised, taxes proposed, the peace treaties re-negotiated with little effect. North was not directly concerned with these measures, and indeed gave little attention even to matters within his own department: 'North was literally and by metaphor the sleeping partner'[18] in the coalition with Fox.

During the remainder of the session the only important challenge to the ministry at Westminster was a motion for parliamentary reform by William Pitt on 7 May. Intended to pinpoint an important subject of disagreement within the administration, it served instead to provide North with a triumph. This was an issue on which only the Northites were united, and with independent support they carried the day by the crushing margin of 293 votes to 149. North used what was to become his stock argument against reform, the lack of popular support for it. The petitions altogether had not more than 20,000 signatures, he said: 'The question in short, now, is, to whom we are to pay respect? The few reformers, or the contented multitude? Can this be a serious question? [There was a great cry of 'Hear him!'] I perceive it cannot.' This debate was also the occasion when North's defence of the existing electoral system was transmuted into a justification of his own career as an answer to Pitt's charge that his ministry had been based on the secret influence of the Crown.[19]

I trust the candid and discerning part of the House will see that the attack is most unjust. I was not, when I was honoured with office, a minister of chance, or a creature of whom Parliament had no experience. I was found among you when I was so honoured. I had long been known to you. In consequence, I obtained your support; when that support was withdrawn, I ceased to be a minister. I was the creature of Parliament in my rise; when I fell I was its victim. I came among you without connection. It was here I was first known, you raised me up, you pulled me down.

The Fox–North coalition knew only too well that any controversial policy or subject might give the King an opportunity to strike at his ministers. During the summer of 1783 they survived one delicate issue, the question of an allowance for the Prince of Wales, a young man of dubious character who was a close friend of Fox and therefore in no way the apple of his father's eye. George III attempted to split the coalition on this point by a vain appeal to North: but his former minister no longer felt the tie of a special relationship with the King. The coalition were unwilling to take further political risks; but there was one nettle that had to be grasped, a problem with which North was only too familiar, India.

Since the stop-gap measures of 1781 the convulsions of the British political scene had prevented any further action by any ministry on the subject: but it was a time when a great deal of information was made known by parliamentary investigation. It became apparent that the problem centred on the lack of effective political control over India from London under the 1773 Act; and the autumn of 1783 saw the ministerial drafting of an India Bill that would put effective power in the hands of a government-nominated Commission of seven M.P.s, who were to hold office for four years. It was primarily the work of Fox and Burke. North had curiously little to do with the formulation and presentation of a measure that fell within his own department and concerned a subject about which he was well informed. This circumstance needs more explanation than that of the inertia customarily suggested when North did nothing: he certainly suffered from bad health during the last months of 1783; but there is also some ground for suspecting that he did have doubts and reservations about the measure. Any private disquiet was concealed by the public approval signified by the fact that his son George seconded Fox's introduction of the bill and was later nominated as one of the Commissioners.

Fox's India Bill was the event that sealed North's political fate. He took little part in the parliamentary discussion of the measure, although on 27 November he spoke with great effect on the second reading, reminding M.P.s that everyone agreed that something had to be done on India and citing precedents for infringement of the Company's charter. In particular he attacked Pitt's charge of confiscation, declaring that Pitt was such 'a great master of words' that in his mouth words 'changed their meaning'. How could it be confiscation when the bill did not lower the dividend, destroy the monopoly or remove any commercial advantages?[20] The bill received a majority that day of 229 votes to 120, and went through the Commons with ease. Neither the propaganda of the Company against interference with chartered rights nor the opposition denunciation of the patronage created by the bill had the impact on parliamentary opinion that they had outside Westminster. It was only the interference of the King that proved decisive in the Lords: and even there his intimidating intimation that any supporter of the bill would be deemed his enemy led to its defeat by a mere eight votes on 15 December. The government case was put so badly that it is not overfanciful to speculate that George III's earlier refusal to give North a peerage had deprived the administration of an able and experienced advocate who might have swayed the division in the bill's favour.[21] All that North could contribute was a powerful exposition of the ministry's case in the Commons debate over the episode on 17 December. Such canvassing by the sovereign against his own ministers would destroy the constitution, North declared: 'The responsibility of ministers was the only security which Englishmen had against the abuse of the executive power.' Obviously sensitive about allegations of Crown influence during his own ministry, North contrasted them with the recent action of the King himself:[22]

What was the influence of the Crown, against which, on former occasions, all these gentlemen had divided against him, and for which he had then deemed it his duty to contend, in comparison of a principle which, once established, would bury, in one grave, all the privileges of Parliament, and the rights of the people?

It was North's last speech as a cabinet minister. Just before eleven o'clock that evening George III sent this note to his Home Secretary: 'Lord North is by this required to send me the Seals of his Department, and to acquaint Mr Fox to send those of the Foreign Department . . . I choose this method as Audiences on such occasions must be unpleasant.' North at once complied with the request.[23]

The King had been able to dismiss the Coalition because Pitt had at last promised to form an administration. Few supporters of Fox and North thought that his ministry would survive in the face of their parliamentary majority; 'the mince-pie administration' one of them dubbed it, unlikely to last long after Christmas. North made a speech in fine fettle on 22 December, waxing sarcastic about a cabinet that then consisted of two members and pointing out the constitutional contrast between the Coalition's accession to office and its removal:[24]

If we became possessed of government, we are at worst charged with having carried it by storm, bravely, in the face of the enemy, not by sap: we carried on our advances regularly, and above ground, in view of the foe, not by mining in the dark, and blowing up the fort before the garrison knew there was an intention to attack it.

North was among those who thought that George III would have to resort to an immediate dissolution. Pitt had indeed accepted office on the assumption that a prompt general election would produce a Commons majority. He had been convinced by an assessment made by North's former election and patronage manager, John Robinson, whose desertion North was not to forgive until his death-bed. During the Christmas recess 'ratcatcher Robinson' sought to make an election unnecessary by the recruitment of parliamentary support from the Coalition majority: but the opposition was also active, with North showing the flag by political dinners. He must have been acutely aware that his own following, many of them accustomed to holding office under the King's government, was more vulnerable to Robinson's seduction than the Foxites. North, with his vast experience of the power of government 'influence', was less optimistic about the parliamentary situation than his younger colleagues: but even he anticipated that the opposition would retain a majority. All calculations soon proved academic when Pitt refused to resign in the face of continuous parliamentary defeats during the first months of 1784.

A solution then much canvassed was an alliance between Pitt and Fox. Since Pitt had repeatedly indicated throughout 1783 that he would never serve with North, the latter made it clear that he would not stand in the way of such an arrangement, telling his father on 24 January that it was 'perfectly well known that my personal claims and interests are no obstacle to any arrangement for the public service'.[25] North expanded on this theme in a debate of 11 February after Pitt had again told the Commons that despite his respect for North's private character and abilities they could never be in the same cabinet. North graciously accepted this veto on office: 'There is no love of power, no love of emolument, no object of ambition, that shall induce me to remain one moment the bar to so great a public benefit as a stable administration.' But he could not forbear to point out that Pitt was defying a Commons majority: 'Let the right Honourable gentleman do what he ought to do to this House, and it is of little comparative importance indeed what becomes of me.'[26] North must have known that there was no real prospect of being called upon to make this self-sacrifice: for the Foxites insisted on the resignation of Pitt before any negotiations took place, and that was a condition neither he nor the King would accept. Their firmness on this point was strengthened by abundant evidence of the coalition's unpopularity in the country. Over 200 counties and towns sent Addresses applauding George III's action; and on 25 February some of the delegates presenting such Addresses at Court hissed North when he was carrying to the throne one of the succession of Commons resolutions calling on the sovereign to dismiss Pitt.

That was an omen that public opinion would reinforce government influence at the forthcoming general election and convert Pitt's anticipated victory into a triumph. When Parliament was dissolved on 26 March abstentions and desertions had already cost the coalition its majority: but a contemporary pamphlet calculation that North still had 112 followers in the Commons throws doubt on Burke's estimate that 54 Northites had gone over to Pitt. Nor did the results of the general election bear out the expectation that North's followers would suffer more losses than those of Fox. Of the 96 coalitionists not returned, only 43 were Northites. The vulnerability of Northites in constituencies under government control or influence was balanced by that of the Foxites in popular constituencies: the upsurge of public opinion was felt even in Banbury, where a Loyal Address from some inhabitants, none of them electors, was followed by a vain attempt to make a challenge to North's candidature. A modern calculation is that altogether 69 Northites survived into the next Parliament.[27]

The constitutional crisis of 1782 to 1784 left North with a tarnished reputation and a ruined career. It is a sorry paradox that he can now be seen to have emerged with great credit both as a politician and as a man. Throughout the period from his resignation he had never wavered in his view of the constitution, his belief that in the end the King should bow to the will of the Commons. He had both left office and returned to it on this principle, and was genuinely indignant when Pitt and George III did not follow the rules of the constitutional game as he understood them. North's character had matched his political integrity. He was big-hearted enough to bear no grudge for years of Foxite attacks. He had refused to desert his ally Fox in the face of royal bullying and blandishments, and had afterwards made no equivalent claim, declaring his willingness to stand aside and present no obstacle to a political solution that would be at his expense. Above all, North's behaviour to his sovereign had been punctilious and helpful in the face of shabby and ungrateful treatment. But George III's regal assumption that North's duty was to serve him when required, no matter what the King had said or done to him, appeared unreasonable even to a man of such sanguine temperament as North.

The King's behaviour over the matter of the 1780 election debt showed him to be at best inconsiderate, at worst spiteful, towards a man who had served him well and faithfully. Nor was it a matter on which he was disposed to change his mind. Henry Drummond, when asked by George III for a loan for the 1784 election campaign, reminded his sovereign that £23,000 was still owing on the previous account. The King therefore instructed Drummond to obtain from North the £17,000 for which he had tacitly accepted responsibility in May 1782. The whole unhappy episode finally came to an end in the autumn of 1784, after North had told Drummond that he could not possibly pay the debt: his private income was £2,500 a year, and the Wardenship of the Cinque Ports yielded less than £3,000. George III was shocked and angry at the news, describing North's conduct to Drummond as 'the most barefaced fraud', and commenting to Robinson that 'this crowns the rest of that Lord's ill behaviour to me and shows that in every line I have equal reason to complain of him': but the King then reluctantly honoured the commitment.[28]

It can be seen in retrospect that North's political career was in one sense at an end after the election of 1784. His chance of returning to office was over. North was soon to be handicapped by ill-health, and always he was saddled with the immense political millstone of the American War. That was a subject to which Pitt and his minions made almost invariable reference in any important debate of the next few years. This complaint about their behaviour by North in 1786 was but one of many: 'The American War was a uniform topic with them. All its disasters were charged on him. In short, the American War was their favourite hobby-horse. They were fond of mounting him on all occasions.'[29]

Yet there was little sign of North's forthcoming political eclipse in the first year of the new Parliament. Still leader of an important party in the Commons, North threw himself into the political battle with great vigour. On 6 July 1784 he roundly condemned Pitt's India Bill as 'a bad Bill', one that would perpetuate the Company's power as long as possible: and he followed this attack by detailed criticisms.[30] Pitt had a safe majority on that measure, but the opposition fared better on other subjects, and North could claim much of the credit for their successes. Pitt was forced to give way on the controversial matter of the Westminster election scrutiny, an attempt to delay or even prevent Fox's return for that constituency, after stormy debates in which North took a prominent part.[31] North also played a major role in the successful attack on Pitt's proposals of 1785 for equality of trade between Ireland and Britain. He underlined the opposition case that Ireland was being favoured at the expense of British industry by contrasting Pitt's plans with his own Irish measures of 1779 and 1780. Stung by Pitt's unfair jibe that he had given away so much to Ireland that there was little worth saving, North rejoined that he had not sacrificed the economic interests of Britain. The 1780 act of generosity admitting Ireland to trade with the British colonies could not give her a claim as of right to free access to the British home market. Later North was not satisfied even with the modified terms introduced by Pitt as a result of British protests and that were in turn to be unacceptable to Ireland. They were no safeguard, North declared on 19 May 1785. Irish manufacturers, with their advantage of cheap labour, would undersell their British rivals: and he added the characteristic point that they would not be contributing to the British tax burden.[32]

These were triumphs shared with his opposition colleagues: but North's most notable success was won on the subject of parliamentary reform, over which he differed from both Pitt and Fox. North had always been the most formidable Commons critic of reform proposals, using the simple argument of the lack of any demand for it. In a reform debate of 16 June 1784 he pointed out that unrepresented towns like Manchester, Leeds and Birmingham had not petitioned: and in a speech said by opponent Sir Edward Astley to be the best he had ever made, North went on to argue that M.P.s were sent to the Commons not to represent districts but to act as trustees for the whole country.[33] In 1785 North chose a different argument to oppose the most famous reform proposal of the decade. On 18 April, Pitt put forward a plan for the voluntary extinction of thirty-six small boroughs by purchase and the transfer of their representation to the counties and to London. This measure North denounced as 'a direct attack on the British constitution . . . If a door was once opened to innovation and experiment, there was no knowing to what extent it might be carried.' He then turned to the familiar theme that the evidence of public demand was pitiful: this time there were only eight petitions. North clinched this point by quoting with great effect what he claimed was a line from *The Rehearsal*, a play written by Lord Buckingham in 1672 and frequently performed in the eighteenth century: 'What horrid sound of *silence* doth assail mine ear!'[34] This cold blast of reality withered the cause of reform. Pitt's modest proposal, although supported by Fox, was rejected by a majority of seventy-four.

North had remained a formidable parliamentary figure even in opposition. His speeches were still adorned with wit and studded with humorous anecdotes. But 1785 marked the end of the high political plateau of his career. Thereafter he went rapidly downhill. Although he remained as cogent as ever in debate, his sparkle vanished under the demoralizing influence of failing health and fading political fortunes. He ceased to attend Parliament regularly, appearing only if subjects of special interest to him were under discussion or when his opposition colleagues had particular need of his debating skill. His personal following in the Commons slowly dwindled, by death, retirement and desertion, the most conspicuous rat being William Eden at the end of 1785. Some forty or more of these former Northites were still in opposition in 1788, but they were becoming indistinguishable from the main opposition party under

Fox: one contemporary calculation of that year gave North under a score of followers, another less than a dozen.

North had largely withdrawn into private life. Contemporary memoirs and family recollections portray his London house in the 1780s as a hive of social activity. North was a man sought after for his company when his power had gone, even though the balance of his moods was now tilting from his customary gaiety to more frequent bouts of melancholy. One depressing circumstance was loss of sight: virtual, soon to be total, blindness descended on him suddenly in 1787. His wife and children had to guide him when walking, read to him, write for him, and help him with his food: Horace Walpole, now a frequent visitor to the North home, reflected in 1787 that 'if ever loss of sight could be compensated it is by so affectionate a family'. Material compensation, too, finally came when his avaricious and domineering father died on 4 August 1790. North became second Earl of Guilford, and inherited estates in five counties. At long last he was free of financial worries.[35]

During these years of semi-retirement the motive that chiefly impelled North to attend the Commons was defence of the existing order in church and state: and it is characteristic of North that he never thought any good would come out of the French Revolution.[36] Many of his best speeches when out of office in the 1780s were made on the theme of resisting change. Already by 1785 he had played the foremost role in checking the Parliamentary Reform movement. The campaign for the abolition of the slave trade was only just gaining momentum, but North had stated his position in a debate of 1783. Although professing sympathy with the aim, he feared that the object was impossible of attainment; the trade was essential to almost every nation and none would abolish it alone.[37] But the most obvious facet of North's conservatism was his vigorous opposition to any attack on the privileged position of the Church of England.

During his ministry North had firmly set his face against any concessions to Dissenters, and he maintained this attitude throughout his life: but although he had the prejudices of a devout Anglican, his arguments both in and out of office were those of state policy. He was prepared to allow non-Anglicans as extensive civil rights as did not threaten church or state, and refused to consider repeal of the Catholic Relief Act of 1778 even after the Gordon Riots of 1780. It was not Catholics but other Protestants who in the later eighteenth century were making sporadic challenges to the Anglican church. On 6 February 1772 North played a leading part in the Commons rejection by 217 votes to 71 of a petition of some 200

Anglican clergy asking for relief from subscription to the Thirty-Nine Articles. In a long speech during which he played on contemporary prejudices against Catholics, Anabaptists and Moslems, North argued that any church would have to impose some test and that acceptance of the petition would admit every 'sectary' into the church.[38] Two years later, on 5 May 1774, North flatly opposed a motion for a Committee on the same subject. It would be rash, improper and dangerous to church and state even to consider any alteration, he said, and the proposal was rejected without a vote.[39] That North was privately nothing like the bigot his public position compelled him to appear was shown by his quiet attempt to remove the Anglican monopoly of Oxford University as soon as he became its Chancellor in October 1772. Although unwilling to become publicly involved, North worked cautiously within the University to remove the test of subscription to the Thirty-Nine Articles that was required prior to matriculation. But his hopes were frustrated by the refusal of the University Convocation to abolish subscription, and when the subject came before the House of Commons in 1773 North felt obliged by his official positions in state and university to oppose a Parliamentary Committee on it.[40]

North was on more difficult ground when countering attempts to give dissenting ministers and schoolmasters legal exemption from penalties for non-subscription to thirty-five of the Thirty-Nine Articles: these penalties had been imposed by seventeenth-century legislation and although not enforced remained on the statute book. On 2 April 1772, the day before Dissenter M.P. Sir Henry Hoghton introduced a bill on this point, George III urged North 'to oppose it personally throughout every stage, which will gain you the applause of the established church and every real friend of the constitution'. North refused to do so, saying that he would thereby incur certain defeat on a matter that would embarrass many of his supporters if a vote was forced.[41] Both then and in 1773 he absented himself from the Commons and relied on the House of Lords to reject the proposed legislation.[42] But when Hoghton proposed the same bill in 1779 North was less inflexible. In Committee on 20 April he introduced a petition from Oxford University asking for some declaration of Christianity instead of subscription to the Anglican Church; and North carried such a clause against the objections of the bill's sponsors, countering Hoghton's argument that conscientious men would not sign the declaration by saying that he saw no need for any change at all, since technical offenders were never prosecuted.[43]

This qualified Relief Act of 1779 did little to assuage the discontent of Dissenters, and in 1787 and 1789 Henry Beaufoy put forward unsuccessful motions for repeal of the Test and Corporation Acts. North made an unwonted effort to attend the debates on them and played a major role in their defeat. On 28 March 1787 he was led into the House by his son George, and made a notable speech even though he was too ill to stay for the vote. North said that the question was not the issue of liberty of conscience that some of the bill's sponsors suggested. The Test Act was 'the great bulwark of the constitution', deliberately left by the Parliament of 1689 as 'a mere civil and political regulation'. He sought to refute the arguments for repeal by denying that the Dissenters suffered indignity; denying that the Anglican clergy favoured repeal so as to prevent their sacrament being used as a political test for state office; and asserting that the plea of birthright also applied to Catholics. 'Let us not, then, confound toleration of religious principles with civil and military appointments . . . The constitution was always in danger when the Church was deprived of its rights.' Pitt, speaking for once on the same side as North, paid him 'the highest compliments', the first he had made since he became minister according to diarist Wraxall.[44] When Beaufoy repeated his motion on 8 May 1789, North was the first to oppose it, announcing that he spoke early since he would not be able to remain long in the House. He deliberately deployed the same arguments as two years before, in case anyone should think he had changed his mind! North ended by expressing the hope that 'he had given offence to no one. He honoured and respected the Dissenters, and was influenced in his opposition only from a conviction, that if the House weakened the Church, they weakened themselves; and that if they abandoned the wise precautions of their ancestors, they endangered the constitution of their country'. He was accused of raising the old Tory cry of 'The Church in danger', and rose to reply that history showed that when the church tottered the state tottered also.[45] This was North's last appearance in the Commons: he was forbidden by his doctor to attend when Fox proposed a similar motion on 2 March 1790.[46]

Apart from such occasions when North felt strongly impelled to give vent to his opinions and prejudices the Commons after 1785 saw little of the man who had been the leading personality there for so long. He made only occasional appearances in the House to buttress the arguments and relieve the embarrassments of his less experienced opposition colleagues. There was indeed one subject that appeared to threaten his alliance with them, the proposed impeachment of Warren Hastings for misgovernment in India. Whereas Burke was pushing this as far and as fast as he was able, and Fox saw political advantage in the subject, North had headed the ministry which had appointed and retained Hastings as Governor-General. He had even formed a political alliance with the Hastings faction during the last years of his administration, and he personally felt that Hastings was entitled by his services to retire with a fortune. Speculation was therefore rife that North would not join in the demand for impeachment. Rumour proved a lying jade, for by the beginning of 1786 the Northites had concurred in impeachment as opposition policy.[47] North felt that there was a case to answer, but he was obviously embarrassed by accusations of inconsistency in the Commons debates of 1786. He defended himself by describing his ministerial relationship with Hastings and emphasizing the abortive attempt to recall the Governor-General in 1776: but he withdrew before the House voted on the prosecution and took no part in the impeachment.[48]

North next briefly emerged from political retirement at the time of the Regency Crisis of 1788–9. In November 1788 George III fell victim to an attack of what was then thought to be insanity but is now known to have been the physical disease of porphyria. His incapacity provoked immediate demands from the opposition that royal power should devolve at once on the Prince of Wales, who as Regent would then dismiss Pitt and appoint Fox in his stead. A great deal of political heat was generated by this demand and by Pitt's riposte of delays and qualifications to the Regent's power. North had not spoken or even appeared in the Commons for eighteen months, but he now answered a summons to repair the damage caused by the extravagant claims made by Fox and his colleagues. North began on 1 December with the bland contention that since everyone was agreed on the choice of the Prince as Regent there should be no disagreement about 'the forms', a specious point that ignored the central controversy over the extent of the Regent's powers: but his chief argument was the need for the immediate restoration of 'the third branch of the legislature'. That was to be North's constant theme. The two Houses alone had no right to pass legislation, and so Pitt's plan for a Regency Bill violated 'the fundamental principles of the constitution'. Parliament should follow the precedent of 1689 and address the Prince of Wales to undertake a Regency during the King's illness. When the bill was introduced North repeatedly attacked both the principle and the details of the proposed restrictions on the power of the Regent.[49] North sought to compensate for the absence of Fox through illness by taking part in almost every debate. Altogether he made two dozen speeches on the subject, and one historian of the episode has described it as 'a moving epilogue to his career'.[50] North returned to political retirement when the crisis dissolved into anticlimax with the King's recovery in February 1789. Rumour said that the first sign of this was George III's comment on overhearing that North had made many inquiries about his health: 'Lord North is a good man, unlike the others. He is a good man.'[51]

North's political career did not end when he succeeded his father in 1790. He made several speeches as second Earl of Guilford, in the role of an opposition leader commenting unfavourably on ministerial policy. Especially did he criticize Pitt's proposed interference on the side of Turkey in her war against Russia, making his maiden speech in the Lords on 1 April 1791 on this subject. The Russian demands on the Ottoman Empire appeared reasonable, North said. Why should Britain risk war merely to alter the terms? What was the value to her of the return of the Black Sea port of Oczakov to the Turks? He forecast that useless expenditure would be the only result of Pitt's policy. One reporter appended this comment: 'The whole of the noble earl's speech was accurate, clear, interesting and eloquent; and from the particular attention with which it was listened to, it seemed to have great effect upon the House.'[52] The Lords had seldom heard such a persuasive speaker as North was, even in the twilight of his career. A year later, when he had been proved right, North mocked the ministerial failure in a debate of 20 February 1792. After all his costly armaments and protracted negotiations, Pitt had accepted the original Russian terms! North then attacked the whole basis of the ministry's foreign policy, claiming that from his own experience in the American War Russia should be cultivated as an ally: 'It was the interest of this country to keep up a good understanding with Russia.'[53]

This piece of wisdom was his last public political pronouncement. His health finally collapsed at the end of July, and he died on 5 August 1792. Accounts of the death-bed scenes have usually been based on the recollections of his daughter Charlotte in 1839: notably that he was thankful for being spared the anarchy and bloodshed he foresaw in France, Britain's traditional foe now being designated 'that unhappy country'; and that he forgave Robinson and Eden for the two political desertions that had upset him.[54] But only eight days later one of Dartmouth's sons had written this more recently discovered description of the final moments:[55]

No man ever met death with greater fortitude. | When he found that he had but few hours to live, he desired that all his family might be sent for to his bedside. When this was done, he said that with regard to his political life, though he could not have the presumption to suppose but what there had been much of error in many things he had done, yet it was a satisfaction which none but himself could in that hour conceive, that on no one act of it could he look back with regret. He then took leave of his family, after thanking them separately for their great kindness and attention to him since the loss of his eyesight, more particularly during his last illness; he expired without a struggle or groan.

Where does North now stand at the bar of history? It is significant that the immediate verdict, at least from informed contemporaries, was not the condemnation North feared in his last days. But as those who had known North died off, and the magnitude of his tasks became obscured by the passage of time, so did North's reputation plummet. He was seen by liberal historians as the conservative opponent of reforms in state and church destined ultimately and rightfully to triumph. He suffered doubly from national prejudices: for Americans he was the man who strove to prevent their independence; in his own country he was the politician who had led Britain to the greatest disaster of modern history. One suspects that even North's appearance has counted against him. His daughter Charlotte remembered that 'his face . . . gave no indication of the brightness of his understanding'.[56] His contemporaries, however, were well aware of the alert mind concealed behind those heavy features. The sharpness publicly displayed in debate was privately known to his colleagues in other ways; Sandwich has left this admiring comment: 'Give Lord North a bundle of papers and he will turn them over once, perhaps while his hair is dressing, and he will instantly know their contents and bearing.'[57]

It is too facile to dismiss as temporary North's achievements at home and abroad.[58] The American War was not the time to solve the long-term problems of Ireland and India. Political solutions are seldom permanent; nor is it always desirable that they should be. The Quebec Act, which came nearest to the permanent settlement of a problem, had to be modified within two decades because of the changing development of Canada. His management of the Treasury was necessarily hand-to-mouth, given the archaic machinery and immense problems. North not only coped efficiently, but developed an attitude to government finance and administration that suggests that, given time, he might have anticipated many of the measures on which the reputation of the Younger Pitt has increasingly come to rest. North's overall record as Prime Minister is such as to justify the claim that although he cannot be acclaimed a great Premier he comes near the top of the second rank.

But that North had so little time of peace as Prime Minister might be deemed his own fault. The American crisis was not a problem he merely inherited. From the Stamp Act onwards North had been closely identified with the British policies that aroused American resistance. It was too late when he tried to draw back from the brink. It was not bad luck but poetic justice that such a man should bear the blame for the loss of America. Others were more extremist in their views, notably some of his colleagues and back-benchers. Nor is there any substantial reason to think that any other politician could or would have averted the catastrophe. But the cold fact remains that North was the man with ultimate political responsibility. To adapt Winston Churchill: North as Prime Minister presided over the dissolution of the First British Empire; and he must pay the historical penalty.

F

REFERENCES

Chapter 1 (pages 1–20)

1. Walpole, *Memoirs, 4,* 52–6.
2. *Glenbervie Diaries, 1,* 61.
3. Brooke, *King George III,* p. 196.
4. *Glenbervie Diaries, 1,* 411. The authenticity of this statement is doubtful. The royal letter on which it is apparently based says only that North had been 'a most faithful First Lord of the Treasury'. Aspinall, *Later Corr. of George III, 4,* 175–6.
5. *North Memoir, 1,* 5. Valentine, *Lord North, 1,* 13–14.
6. Lucas, *Lord North, 1,* 22.
7. Valentine, *Lord North, 1,* 22.
8. Valentine, *Lord North, 1,* 9. Dated by internal evidence as 1740.
9. Valentine, *Lord North, 1,* 74–5.

10. Valentine, *Lord North, 1,* 28–9.
11. Brougham, *Historical Sketches,* p. 392.
12. Pemberton, *Lord North,* pp. 20–25. Valentine, *Lord North, 1,* 28–9, 75–6, 80–82, 104, 109–10, 128–9.
13. *North Memoir, 1,* 7–8.
14. Valentine, *Lord North, 1,* 78.
15. Pemberton, *Lord North,* p. 23.
16. Lucas, *Lord North, 1,* 29.
17. B.L. Add. MSS 32919, fos. 1–2; 32933, fo. 176.
18. B.L. Add. MSS 32933, fo. 183.
19. *Glenbervie Diaries, 1,* 7. *Bute Letters,* pp. 159, 176.
20. Thomas, *British Politics and the Stamp Act Crisis,* p. 6.
21. *Grenville Papers, 2,* 133.
22. *Grenville Papers, 2,* 151–3, 209.
23. *North Memoir, 1,* 9.
24. Walpole, *Memoirs, 1,* 257–8.
25. There is a full account of the Commons debates on the *North Briton* case in Tomlinson, Thesis, pp. 48–102.
26. Walpole, *Memoirs, 2,* 32. *Chatham Papers, 2,* 303. Valentine, *Lord North, 1,* 134.
27. *Ryder Diary,* pp. 244, 252.
28. *Grenville Papers, 3,* 27n.
29. *Cavendish Debates, 1,* 299. *Ryder Diary,* pp. 258–9.
30. Tomlinson, *Additional Grenville Papers,* pp. 205–6.
31. Fortescue, *Corr. of George III, 1,* 126, 131, 154.
32. B.L. Add. MSS 32972, fo. 25.
33. *H.M.C Dartmouth, 3,* 179–80.
34. Fortescue, *Corr. of George III, 1,* 205, 236. *Ryder Diary,* pp. 280, 315.
35. Lucas, *Lord North, 1,* 36–7. Fortescue, *Corr. of George III, 1,* 309. *Jenkinson Papers,* p. 410.
36. *North Memoir, 1,* 9.
37. *Jenkinson Papers,* p. 420. *Glenbervie Diaries, 1,* 170. *North Memoir, 1,* 10.
38. *Ryder Diary,* p. 334.
39. *Grafton Autobiography,* pp. 122–3. Fortescue, *Corr. of George III, 1,* 459–60. *Glenbervie Diaries, 1,* 166. *Burke Corr., 1,* 298.
40. Walpole, *Memoirs, 2,* 298. *Ryder Diary,* pp. 332–3.
41. Walpole, *Memoirs, 3,* 115. *Ryder Diary,* p. 345.
42. *North Memoir, 1,* 11.

Chapter 2 (pages 21–37)

1. *Trumbull Papers,* p. 246.
2. *Grafton Autobiography,* pp. 166–8. For detailed accounts of the episode, see Valentine, *Lord North, 1,* 152–8; and Brown, Thesis, pp. 10–21.
3. *Grafton Autobiography,* p. 227. Walpole, *Memoirs, 3,* 90. *Grenville Papers, 4,* 304.
4. *North Memoir, 1,* 13.
5. B.L. Add. MSS 32987, fos. 301–2. *Grenville Papers, 4,* 194. *Burke Corr., 1,* 342, 345.

6. *Grafton Autobiography*, p. 227.
7. Fortescue, *Corr. of George III*, *2*, 21.
8. B.L. Add. MSS 32990, fo. 71.
9. *Cavendish Debates*, *1*, 21–2, 27–8.
10. Hughes, *E.H.R.*, 62 (1947), p. 219.
11. *Grafton Autobiography*, pp. 227–8.
12. *Cavendish Debates*, *1*, 120–38.
13. Fortescue, *Corr. of George III*, *2*, 76.
14. *Cavendish Debates*, *1*, 151–85.
15. Fortescue, *Corr. of George III*, *2*, 79.
16. *Cavendish Debates*, *1*, 227–37.
17. *Cavendish Debates*, *1*, 345–55.
18. *Cavendish Debates*, *1*, 360–86.
19. Fortescue, *Corr. of George III*, *2*, 90.
20. Fortescue, *Corr. of George III*, *2*, 91.
21. *Cavendish Debates*, *1*, 240–51.
22. *Cavendish Debates*, *1*, 267–306.
23. *Cavendish Debates*, *1*, 251–67.
24. *Trumbull Papers*, p. 303. North did not deny this statement when confronted with it by Barré on 26 Jan. 1769. *Trumbull Papers*, pp. 313–14. *Cavendish Debates*, *1*, 206–7.
25. *Cavendish Debates*, *1*, 84, 88–9.
26. *Cavendish Debates*, *1*, 190–207.
27. *Cavendish Debates*, *1*, 391–401.
28. *Grafton Autobiography*, pp. 229–30.
29. *Grafton Autobiography*, p. 234.
30. Fortescue, *Corr. of George III*, *2*, 110. *North Memoir*, *1*, 16. For the collapse of the Grafton ministry I have relied primarily on Hamer, Thesis, pp. 132–59.
31. B.L. Egerton MSS 3711, pp. 1–61.
32. Fortescue, *Corr. of George III*, *2*, 126.
33. B.L.Egerton MSS 3711, pp. 106–73.
34. Elliot, *Border Elliots*, pp. 406–7.
35. B.L. Egerton MSS 3711, pp. 173–246. Walpole, *Memoirs*, *4*, 50–52. Fortescue, *Corr. of George III*, *2*, 128.
36. *Cavendish Debates*, *1*, 442–58.
37. Thomas, *House of Commons*, pp. 279–80.
38. *Cavendish Debates*, *1*, 458–83.
39. Hamer, Thesis, p. 189.

Chapter 3 (pages 38–67)

1. For some examples see Christie, *Myth and Reality*, pp. 88–91.
2. *Hutchinson Diary*, *1*, 480.
3. *Hutchinson Diary*, *1*, 404, 444.
4. *London Evening Post*, 27 Jan. 1770, quoted in Thomas, *House of Commons*, p. 232.
5. Almon, *Parl. Reg.*, *1*, 33–4.
6. *Cavendish Debates*, *2*, 80.
7. *Glenbervie Diaries*, *1*, 237–8.
8. Valentine, *Lord North*, *2*, 432.

9. *Glenbervie Diaries*, *1*, 87, 326.
10. For an exposition of North's debating techniques see Smith, *Q.J.S.*, 45 (1959), 29–38.
11. *Cavendish Debates*, *2*, 85.
12. B.L. Egerton MSS 258, pp. 79–80.
13. *Glenbervie Diaries*, *1*, 149, 326.
14. *London Evening Post*, 25 Feb. 1772. This story is confirmed by Walpole, *Last Journals*, *1*, 21–2. Seymour's complaint was over what he had thought a promise of Parliamentary support, not of patronage; but North was evidently explaining his usual technique of refusal.
15. Johnson, *E.H.R.*, 89 (1974), 759–64, 776–81.
16. Walpole, *Last Journals*, *1*, 22 n.
17. Brown, Thesis, pp. 113–17.
18. *Hutchinson Diary*, *1*, 454.
19. B.L. Add. MSS 35609, fo. 169.
20. Fortescue, *Corr. of George III*, *3*, 75–6.
21. *Hutchinson Diary*, *1*, 378.
22. Fortescue, *Corr. of George III*, *3*, 479–80. Valentine, *Lord North*, *1*, 459–60. I know of no precise calculation of North's official income: but that of Pitt from the same sources in the next decade has been estimated at a net £6,900. Ehrman, *Younger Pitt*, pp. 595–6.
23. *Cavendish Debates*, *2*, 352–77.
24. For the British reaction I have relied on Hamer, Thesis, pp. 202–43.
25. *Sandwich Papers*, *1*, 12–14.
26. Fortescue, *Corr. of George III*, *2*, 172–82.
27. Fortescue, *Corr. of George III*, *2*, 171, 174, 183–6.
28. Fortescue, *Corr. of George III*, *2*, 204–11. *Grafton Autobiography*, pp. 260–61.
29. *Cavendish Debates*, *2*, 37–54.
30. B.L. Add. MSS 35609, fos. 266–7.
31. *Cavendish Debates*, *2*, 57–88.
32. *Cavendish Debates*, *2*, 217–26, 231–42.
33. *Cavendish Debates*, *2*, 272–306.
34. Fortescue, *Corr. of George III*, *2*, 251–4.
35. Fortescue, *Corr. of George III*, *2*, 252–3. *Grafton Autobiography*, p. 264.
36. For this episode see Brown, Thesis, pp. 159–69; Hamer, Thesis, pp. 300–25; and Marshall, *E.H.R.*, 80 (1965), pp. 717–39.
37. Fortescue, *Corr. of George III*, *2*, 368–70, 376.
38. Bargar, *Dartmouth*, pp. 56–7.
39. *Cavendish Debates*, *1*, 300.
40. For this episode see Thomas, *B.I.H.R.*, 33 (1960), pp. 86–98.
41. North's peacetime Budget Days took place on 8 Feb. 1768, 10 April 1769, 25 April 1770, 10 April 1771, 1 May 1772, 14 June 1773, 18 May 1774, 2 May 1775. The formal proposals may be found in the *Commons Journals* for the report stage, usually the next day. North's Budget speeches and any ensuing debates may be found in the reports listed in Thomas, *Sources for Debates of the House of Commons 1768–1774*. For an account of Budget Day at this time see Thomas, *House of Commons*, pp. 78–81.

F*

42. *Bedford Papers, 3*, 408.
43. Fortescue, *Corr. of George III, 2*, 140–41.
44. *Sandwich Papers, 1*, 20–21.
45. Almon, *Parl. Reg., 1*, 446–56.
46. *Cavendish Debates, 1*, 552–60.
47. Cobbett, *Parliamentary History, 20*, 269–71. Almon, *Parliamentary Register, 11*, 22, 133.
48. *Chatham Corr., 4*, 238–9.
49. Brickdale Diary, *1*, 1–16.
50. Brickdale Diary, *1*, 22–6.
51. B.L. Add. MSS 35504, fo. 170.
52. Brickdale Diary, *8*, 27–9.
53. Brickdale Diary, *8*, 49–50.
54. Brickdale Diary, *8*, 63–91.
55. B.L. Add. MSS 35504, fos. 268–9.
56. B.L. Egerton MSS 249, pp. 11–46.
57. Brickdale Diary, *9*, 13–19.
58. Brickdale Diary, *9*, 5–9.
59. Quoted in Marshall, *Problems of Empire*, p. 34.

Chapter 4 (pages 68–92)

1. *Cavendish Debates, 1*, 483–500.
2. *Cavendish Debates, 1*, 548–62; B.L. Add. MSS 35609, fos. 176–7; Egerton MSS 222, pp. A62–8.
3. *Cavendish Debates, 2*, 14–37.
4. Dickerson, *N.E.Q., 31* (1958), 240–41.
5. *Hutchinson Diary, 1*, 181.
6. B.L. Egerton MSS 246, pp. 1–16.
7. *Hutchinson Diary, 1*, 181–2.
8. *H.M.C. Knox*, p. 257.
9. Brickdale Diary, *10*, 16–23.
10. Brickdale Diary, *10*, 38.
11. *Burke Corr., 2*, 528.
12. B.L. Egerton MSS 256, pp. 109–303; 257, pp. 1–37.
13. B.L. Egerton MSS 257, pp. 123–42.
14. *Hutchinson Diary, 1*, 181–2.
15. B.L. Egerton MSS 260, pp. 12–24.
16. B.L. Egerton MSS 260, pp. 149–56.
17. B.L. Egerton MSS 259, pp. 149–214; 260, pp. 166–9; 262, pp. 133–4.
18. *Hutchinson Diary, 1*, 203.
19. *Hutchinson Diary, 1*, 184, 201, 211–12, 245.
20. Fortescue, *Corr. of George III, 3*, 133–4.
21. *Hutchinson Diary, 1*, 298.
22. Fortescue, *Corr. of George III, 3*, 152–3.
23. *Hutchinson Diary, 1*, 293, 297, 329–30.
24. *Hutchinson Diary, 1*, 299–300.
25. Fortescue, *Corr. of George III, 3*, 156.
26. *H.M.C. Dartmouth, 1*, 372–3.
27. *Hutchinson Diary, 1*, 212.

28. Fortescue, *Corr. of George III, 3*, 177.
29. *Hutchinson Diary, 1*, 315. Almon, *Parl. Reg., 1*, 4–6.
30. Almon, *Parl. Reg., 1*, 132–41. *Hutchinson Diary, 1*, 367–8.
31. Almon, *Parl. Reg., 1*, 169.
32. Almon, *Parl. Reg., 1*, 171–8.
33. *Hutchinson Diary, 1*, 399–400. Fortescue, *Corr. of George III, 3*, 178.
34. Almon, *Parl. Reg., 1*, 195–214.
35. *Hutchinson Diary, 1*, 400.
36. Almon, *Parl. Reg., 1*, 374.
37. *Hutchinson Diary, 1*, 445.
38. Almon, *Parl. Reg., 1*, 467–78.
39. *Hutchinson Diary, 1*, 460, 471.
40. Fortescue, *Corr. of George III, 3*, 234.
41. Hughes, *E.H.R.*, 60 (1947), pp. 228–9.
42. Fortescue, *Corr. of George III, 3*, 277–87.
43. *Grafton Autobiography*, p. 273.
44. *Hutchinson Diary, 1*, 555.
45. Almon, *Parl. Reg., 3*, 1–44.
46. Almon, *Parl. Reg., 3*, 195–8, 236.
47. *H.M.C. Knox*, p. 259.

Chapter 5 (*pages* 93–111)

1. For British foreign policy at this time see Roberts, *Splendid Isolation 1763–1780*.
2. For what follows see Mackesy, *War for America*, pp. 165–75.
3. *Sandwich Papers, 1*, 19–23.
4. Fortescue, *Corr. of George III, 3*, 429–31.
5. Mackesy, *War for America*, pp. 315–16, 371–2, 377–9. Madariaga, *Armed Neutrality*, pp. 121–4, 182, 239–42, 283–302.
6. Fortescue, *Corr. of George III, 4*, 70.
7. Butterfield, *C.H.J.*, 5 (1937), 268.
8. On this subject see Baker, *Government and Contractors*.
9. Almon, *Parl. Reg., 7*, 210–14.
10. Syrett, *Shipping and the American War*, pp. 121–38.
11. For details and discussions of North's wartime finance I have used the *Commons Journals* and the following reports of debates: Almon, *Parl. Reg., 3*, 499–91*; *7*, 182–93, 199–217; *9*, 1–6; *12*, 4–10, 12–23; *13*, 150–51, 178–87; *17*, 200–210, 337–46: Debrett, *Parl. Reg.*, *2*, 179–218, 224–56; *6*, 284–309, 412–43. Budget and other relevant debates took place on these dates: 24 April 1776; 14 May 1777; 9 March 1778; 24 Feb., 1 March, 26 and 31 May 1779; 6 and 15 March 1780; 7, 8, 12, 14 March 1781; 25, 26 Feb., 11 March 1782.
12. Fortescue, *Corr. of George III, 4*, 76.
13. Debrett, *Parl. Reg., 3*, 280–94.
14. Norris, *Shelburne and Reform*. Ehrman, *The Younger Pitt*.
15. *Sandwich Papers, 2*, 255.
16. Fortescue, *Corr. of George III, 3*, 421–2, 427–31.
17. Ritcheson, *British Politics and the American Revolution*, p. 233.
18. Fortescue, *Corr. of George III, 4*, 26–31.
19. Almon, *Parl. Reg., 8*, 379–432.

20. Fortescue, *Corr. of George III*, *4*, 77, 350.
21. *Sandwich Papers*, *1*, 347.
22. Wraxall, *Memoirs*, *2*, 435.

Chapter 6 (*pages* 112–32)

1. Fortescue, *Corr. of George III*, *4*, 220.
2. Fortescue, *Corr. of George III*, *3*, 478–9; *6*, 7.
3. Almon, *Parl. Reg.*, *6*, 33–6.
4. Fortescue, *Corr. of George III*, *4*, 54–88.
5. Almon, *Parl. Reg.*, *8*, 337, 360.
6. Fortescue, *Corr. of George III*, *4*, 214–15.
7. Almon, *Parl. Reg.*, *12*, 23–52.
8. *H.M.C. Knox*, pp. 260–61, 267. *Sandwich Papers*, *3*, 26.
9. Butterfield, *C.H.J.*, 5 (1937), p. 267.
10. Almon, *Parl. Reg.*, *9*, 97, 118–23, 136–7, 162–3, 173–94, 200, 242–3.
11. Almon, *Parl. Reg.*, *11*, 218–20, 237–8; *12*, 108–9; *13*, 151. Cobbett, *Parl. Hist.*, *20*, 136–8, 248–50.
12. Butterfield, *George III, Lord North and the People*, pp. 117–38. Valentine, *Lord North*, *2*, 135–57.
13. Almon, *Parl. Reg.*, *16*, 21–2.
14. Almon, *Parl. Reg.*, *16*, 174–87; *17*, 56–63, 68, 82–3.
15. *H.M.C. Stopford-Sackville*, *1*, 264.
16. Christie, *Wilkes, Wyvill and Reform*, pp. 68–115.
17. Almon, *Parl. Reg.*, *17*, 92, 116, 119–22, 131–2, 137–8, 156–61, 190–92, 254–78, 297–337, 374–86.
18. Almon, *Parl. Reg.*, *17*, 440–74.
19. Fortescue, *Corr. of George III*, *5*, 39–40.
20. Almon, *Parl. Reg.*, *17*, 534–67.
21. *Glenbervie Diaries*, *1*, 306.
22. Christie, *End of North's Ministry*, pp. 1–46. Valentine, *Lord North*, *2*, 215–31.
23. Christie, *End of North's Ministry*, pp. 46–230.
24. Christie, *End of North's Ministry*, pp. 231–66.
25. Almon, *Parl. Reg.*, *17*, 388–97.
26. Sutherland, *East India Company*, pp. 269–364.
27. Debrett, *Parl. Reg.*, *5*, 32–5.
28. Debrett, *Parl. Reg.*, *5*, 124.
29. Wraxall, *Memoirs*, *2*, 467–8.
30. Fortescue, *Corr. of George III*, *5*, 326–7.
31. Christie, *End of North's Ministry*, pp. 267–83.
32. Fortescue, *Corr. of George III*, *5*, 336–7.
33. Christie, *End of North's Ministry*, pp. 283–98.
34. Wraxall, *Memoirs*, *2*, 134–6.
35. Fortescue, *Corr. of George III*, *5*, 375–6.
36. Christie, *End of North's Ministry*, pp. 299–339.
37. Fortescue, *Corr. of George III*, *5*, 377–80.
38. Fortescue, *Corr. of George III*, *5*, 394–7.
39. Walpole, *Last Journals*, *2*, 422.
40. Wraxall, *Memoirs*, *2*, 607. Valentine, *Lord North*, *2*, 315–16.

Chapter 7 (*pages* 133–53)

1. Valentine, *Lord North*, *2*, 321, states that North was offered and refused a peerage; but the sources cited do not bear out this interpretation.
2. Fortescue, *Corr. of George III*, *6*, 27.
3. Christie, *Myth and Reality*, pp. 183–90.
4. Fortescue, *Corr. of George III*, *6*, 97–8.
5. Cannon, *Fox-North Coalition*, p. 29.
6. Cobbett, *Parl. Hist.*, *23*, 249–61.
7. Cobbett, *Parl. Hist.*, *23*, 316–9.
8. *Burke Corr.*, *5*, 56.
9. *Fox Memoirs*, *2*, 30.
10. For some complaints by North of Pitt's behaviour see Cobbett, *Parl. Hist.*, *25*, 588–91, 1402.
11. *Fox Memorials*, *2*, 31–5.
12. *Fox Memorials*, *2*, 38.
13. Cobbett, *Parl. Hist.*, *23*, 518–19, 556–60.
14. *Glenbervie Diaries*, *1*, 180, 388–9.
15. Cobbett, *Parl. Hist.*, *23*, 443–55.
16. Cannon, *Fox-North Coalition*, pp. 54–8.
17. Fortescue, *Corr. of George III*, *6*, 257–8, 260–61, 262.
18. Lucas, *Lord North*, *2*, 240.
19. Cobbett, *Parl. Hist.*, *23*, 847–61.
20. Cobbett, *Parl. Hist.*, *23*, 1283–6.
21. This suggestion is made by Cannon, *Fox-North Coalition*, pp. 137–8.
22. Cobbett, *Parl. Hist.*, *24*, 199, 203–5.
23. Fortescue, *Corr. of George III*, *6*, 476–7.
24. Cobbett, *Parl. Hist.*, *24*, 254–8.
25. Valentine, *Lord North*, *2*, 404.
26. Cobbett, *Parl. Hist.*, *24*, 589–92.
27. Cannon, *Fox-North Coalition*, pp. 216–28. An estimate of only 51 is made by O'Gorman, *Whig Party and the French Revolution*, pp. 245–6.
28. Aspinall, *Later Corr. of George III*, *1*, 42–3, 47, 80–81, 89, 95, 105–6. Christie, *Myth and Reality*, pp. 192–5.
29. Cobbett, *Parl. Hist.*, *25*, 1044.
30. Cobbett, *Parl. Hist.*, *24*, 1142–3, 1167, 1202–9.
31. Cobbett, *Parl. Hist.*, *24*, 820–22, 880–81; *25*, 30–31, 44–6, 100–101.
32. Cobbett, *Parl. Hist.*, *25*, 328–30, 588–91, 632–44, 678–9, 720–5.
33. Cobbett, *Parl. Hist.*, *24*, 987–92.
34. Debrett, *Parl. Reg.*, *18*, 64–70. Wraxall, *Memoirs*, *5*, 294, also noted North's attribution. But a perusal of the play has failed to reveal the line, and it has been deemed a misquotation from Dryden by Lucas, *Lord North*, *2*, 287.
35. Valentine, *Lord North*, *2*, 442–7.
36. *Glenbervie Diaries*, *1*, 154.
37. Cobbett, *Parl. Hist.*, *23*, 1026–7.
38. B.L. Egerton MSS 232, pp. 155–69.
39. B.L. Egerton MSS 257, pp. 86–9, 113.
40. B.L. Egerton MSS 244, pp. 222–31. For the Oxford episode see Brown, Thesis, pp. 87–91.

41. Fortescue, *Corr. of George III*, *2*, 334–6.
42. B.L. Egerton MSS 233, pp. 204–22; 243, pp. 282–407: Add. MSS 35610, fos. 185, 199.
43. Almon, *Parl. Reg.*, *12*, 100–108, 308–18, 353–4.
44. Cobbett, *Parl. Hist.*, *26*, 818–23. Wraxall, *Memoirs*, *6*, 285–7.
45. Cobbett, *Parl. Hist.*, *28*, 16–27.
46. *The Public Advertiser*, 8 March 1790. I owe this reference to Mr M. Fitzpatrick.
47. Marshall, *Impeachment of Warren Hastings*, pp. 38, 185.
48. Cobbett, *Parl. Hist.*, *25*, 1080–81; *26*, 45–7; *29*, 537–9. Wraxall, *Memoirs*, *5*, 141–3.
49. Cobbett, *Parl. Hist.*, *27*, 749–52, 830–34, 950–60, 1014, 1020–23, 1039–40, 1140–44, 1148, 1180, 1187–8, 1195, 1199–1202, 1205–7, 1209–10, 1218–19, 1222, 1224, 1225, 1226, 1228.
50. Derry, *Regency Crisis*, p. 98.
51. Wraxall, *Memoirs*, *7*, 315–16.
52. Cobbett, *Parl. Hist.*, *29*, 86–93.
53. Cobbett, *Parl. Hist.*, *29*, 855–60.
54. Brougham, *Historical Sketches*, pp. 396–7.
55. Aspinall, *Later Corr. of George III*, *1*, 604 n.
56. Brougham, *Historical Sketches*, pp. 391–2.
57. Valentine, *Lord North*, *2*, 464.
58. cf. Valentine, *Lord North*, *2*, 468.

BIBLIOGRAPHY

PRIMARY SOURCES

A. *Manuscripts*

The Parliamentary Diary of Matthew Brickdale 1770–74. 11 vols. Bristol University Library.

The Parliamentary Diary of Henry Cavendish 1768–74. B[ritish] L[ibrary] Egerton MSS 215–63, 3711.

Newcastle Papers. B.L. Add. MSS 32679–33201.

Hardwicke Papers. B.L. Add. MSS 35349–36278.

B. *Printed Sources*

   i. *Parliamentary Proceedings*

Journals of the House of Commons

Almon, John, *The Parliamentary Register . . . 1774 to 1780.* London, 17 vols., 1775–80. Cited as Almon, *Parl. Reg.*

Cobbett, William, *Parliamentary History of England from* . . . . *1066 to* . . . *1803*. London, 36 vols., 1806–20. Cited as Cobbett, *Parl. Hist.*

Debrett, John, *The Parliamentary Register* . . . *1780 to 1796*. London, 45 vols., 1781–96. Cited as Debrett, *Parl. Reg.*

ii. *Correspondence, Diaries and Memoirs*

Historical Manuscripts Commission (cited as *H.M.C.*)
9 Report, Part III, Stopford Sackville MSS., 1884.
Dartmouth MSS., 3 vols., 1887–96.
Various MSS. VI, Knox MSS., 1906.

Russell, Lord John, ed., *Correspondence of John, fourth Duke of Bedford, selected from the originals at Woburn Abbey*. London, Longmans Green, 3 vols., 1842–6. Cited as *Bedford Papers*.

Copeland, T.W. and others, ed., *The Correspondence of Edmund Burke*, 9 vols. Cambridge University Press, 1958–70. Cited as *Burke Corr.*

Sedgwick, R., ed., *Letters from George III to Lord Bute 1756–1766*. London, Macmillan, 1939. Cited as *Bute Letters*.

Wright, J., ed., *Sir Henry Cavendish's Debates of the House of Commons during the Thirteenth Parliament of Great Britain*, 2 vols. London, Longmans Green, 1841–3. Cited as *Cavendish Debates*.

Taylor, W.S. and Pringle, J.H., eds., *Correspondence of William Pitt, Earl of Chatham*, 4 vols. London, Murray, 1838–40.

Russell, Lord John, ed., *Memorials and Correspondence of Charles James Fox*, 4 vols. London, Bentley, 1853.

Fortescue, Sir John, ed., *The Correspondence of King George the Third from 1760 to December 1783*, 6 vols. London, Macmillan, 1928.

Aspinall, A., ed., *The Later Correspondence of George III*, 5 vols. Cambridge University Press, 1966–70.

Bickley, F., ed., *The Diaries of Sylvester Douglas, Lord Glenbervie*, 2 vols. London, Constable, 1928. Cited as *Glenbervie Diaries*.

Anson, Sir William R., ed., *Autobiography and Political Correspondence of Augustus Henry, Third Duke of Grafton*. London, Murray, 1898.

Smith, W.J., ed., *The Grenville Papers: being the correspondence of Richard Grenville, Earl Temple, K.G., and the Right Hon. George Grenville, their friends and contemporaries*, 4 vols. London, Murray, 1852–3.

Tomlinson, J., ed., *Additional Grenville Papers 1763–65*. Manchester University Press, 1962.

Hutchinson, P.O., ed., *The Diary and Letters of his Excellency Thomas Hutchinson, Esq.*, 2 vols. London, Sampson Low, 1883–6. Cited as *Hutchinson Diary*.

Jucker, N.S., ed., *The Jenkinson Papers 1760–1766*. London, Macmillan, 1949.

Thomas, P.D.G., ed., 'The Parliamentary Diaries of Nathaniel Ryder 1764–1767', *Camden Miscellany XXIII*. London, Royal Historical Society, Camden Fourth Series, vol. VII, 1969. Cited as *Ryder Diary*.

Barnes, G.R. and Owen, J.H., eds., *The Private Papers of John Montagu, Fourth Earl of Sandwich, 1771–1782*, 4 vols. London, Navy Records Society, 1932–8. Cited as *Sandwich Papers*.

'Letters of William Samuel Johnson to the Governors of Connecticut', *Trumbull Papers*. Boston, Massachusetts Historical Society, Fifth Series, 9 (1855). Cited as *Trumbull Papers*.

Barker, G.F. Russell, ed., *Horace Walpole. Memoirs of the Reign of King George the Third*, 4 vols. London, Lawrence and Bullen, 1894. Cited as Walpole, *Memoirs*.

Steuart, A.F., ed., *The Last Journals of Horace Walpole, during the Reign of George III from 1771–1783*. 2 vols. London, Bodley Head, 1910. Cited as Walpole, *Last Journals*.

Historical and Posthumous Memoirs of his own time by Sir N.W. Wraxall, Bart, 7 vols. London, Richard Bentley, 1836. Cited as Wraxall, *Memoirs*.

SECONDARY SOURCES

A. *Books*

Baker, N., *Government and Contractors: the British Treasury and War Supplies, 1775–1783*. London, Athlone Press, 1971.

Bargar, B.D., *Lord Dartmouth and the American Revolution*. Columbia, University of South Carolina Press, 1965.

Binney, J.E.D., *British Public Finance and Administration 1774–92*. Oxford, Clarendon Press, 1958.

Brooke, J., *The Chatham Administration 1766–1768*. London, Macmillan, 1956.

Brooke, J., *King George III*. London, Constable, 1972.

Brougham, Henry Lord, *Historical Sketches of Statesmen who flourished in the time of George III*. London, Charles Knight and Co., 1839. 2 vols.

Brown, G.S., *The American Secretary: the Colonial Policy of Lord George Germain, 1775–1778*. Ann Arbor, University of Michigan Press, 1963.

Butterfield, H., *George III, Lord North and the People 1779–80*. London, G. Bell, 1949.

Cannon, J., *The Fox-North Coalition: Crisis of the Constitution 1782–4*. Cambridge University Press, 1969.

Cannon, J. *Lord North: The Noble Lord in the Blue Ribbon*. London, The Historical Association, General Series Pamphlet No. 74, 1970.

Christie, I.R., *The End of North's Ministry 1780–1782*. London, Macmillan, 1958.

Christie, I.R., *Wilkes, Wyvill and Reform: the Parliamentary Reform Movement in British Politics 1760–1785*. London, Macmillan, 1962.

Christie, I.R., *Myth and Reality in Late-Eighteenth Century British Politics and Other Papers*. London, Macmillan, 1970.

Derry, J.W., *The Regency Crisis and the Whigs 1788–9*. Cambridge University Press, 1963.

Donoughue, B., *British Politics and the American Revolution: the Path to War 1773–75*. London, Macmillan, 1964.

Ehrman, J., *The Younger Pitt: the Years of Acclaim*. London, Constable, 1969.

Elliot, G.F.S., *The Border Elliots and the Family of Minto*. Edinburgh, privately printed, 1897.

Fitzmaurice, Lord, *Life of William Earl of Shelburne, afterwards First Marquess of Lansdowne*. London, Macmillan, 1912. 2 vols.

Gruber, I.D., *The Howe Brothers and the American Revolution*. New York, Atheneum Press, 1972.

Hoffman, R.J.S., *The Marquis: A Study of Lord Rockingham 1730–1782*. New York, Fordham University Press, 1973.

Johnston, E.M., *Great Britain and Ireland, 1760–1800*. Edinburgh, Oliver and Boyd, 1963.

Kemp, B., *Sir Francis Dashwood: An Eighteenth Century Independent*. London, Macmillan, 1967.

Labaree, B.W., *The Boston Tea Party*. New York, Oxford University Press, 1964.

Langford, P., *The First Rockingham Administration 1765–1766*. London, Oxford University Press, 1973.

Lucas, R., *Lord North, Second Earl of Guilford, 1732–1792*. London, Arthur L. Humphreys, 1913. 2 vols.

Mackesy, P., *The War for America 1775–1783*. London, Longmans, 1964.

Madariaga, I.D., *Britain, Russia and the Armed Neutrality of 1780*. London, Hollis and Carter, 1962.

Marshall, P.J., *The Impeachment of Warren Hastings*. London, Oxford University Press, 1965.

Marshall, P.J., *Problems of Empire: Britain and India 1757–1813*. London, Allen and Unwin, 1968.

Mitchell, L.G., *Charles James Fox and the Disintegration of the Whig Party 1782–1794*. London, Oxford University Press, 1971.

Namier, Sir Lewis and Brooke, J., eds., *The House of Commons 1754–1790: the History of Parliament*. London, H.M.S.O., 1964. 3 vols.

Norris, J., *Shelburne and Reform*. London, Macmillan, 1963.

North, Lord, *Lord North, the Prime Minister. A Personal Memoir*. London, Heinemann, 1899 and 1903.

O'Connell, M.R., *Irish Politics and Social Conflict in the Age of the American Revolution*. Philadelphia, University of Pennsylvania Press, 1965.

O'Gorman, F., *The Whig Party and the French Revolution*. London, Macmillan, 1967.

Pemberton, W.B., *Lord North*. London, Longmans, Green and Co., 1938.

Ritcheson, C.R., *British Politics and the American Revolution*. Norman, University of Oklahoma Press, 1954.

Roberts, M., *Splendid Isolation 1763–1780*. University of Reading Press, 1970.

Roseveare, H., *The Treasury: The Evolution of a British Institution*. London, Allen Lane, 1969.

Sutherland, L.S., *The East India Company in Eighteenth Century Politics*. Oxford, Clarendon Press, 1952.

Syrett, D., *Shipping and the American War 1775–83. A Study of British Transport Organisation*. London, Athlone Press, 1970.

Thomas, P.D.G., *The House of Commons in the Eighteenth Century*. Oxford, Clarendon Press, 1971.

Thomas, P.D.G., *British Politics and the Stamp Act Crisis: The First Phase of the American Revolution, 1763–1767*. Oxford, Clarendon Press, 1975.

Valentine, A., *Lord North*. Norman, University of Oklahoma Press, 1967. 2 vols.

Van Thal, H., ed., *The Prime Ministers. Volume the First. From Sir Robert Walpole to Sir Robert Peel*. London, Allen and Unwin, 1974.

B. *Periodical Publications*

Anderson, M.S., 'Great Britain and the Russo-Turkish War of 1768–74', *English Historical Review, 69*, 1954.

Beckett, J.C., 'Anglo-Irish constitutional relations in the later eighteenth century', *Irish Historical Studies, 14*, 1964.

Brown, G.S., 'The Anglo-French naval crisis of 1778: a study of conflict', *William and Mary Quarterly*, Third Series, *13*, 1956.

Butterfield, H., 'Lord North and Mr. Robinson, 1779', *Cambridge Historical Journal, 5*, 1935–7.

Christie, I.R., 'The Marquis of Rockingham and Lord North's offer of a coalition, June-July 1780', *English Historical Review, 69*, 1954.

Christie, I.R., 'George III and the debt on Lord North's election account 1780–84', *English Historical Review, 78*, 1963.

Dickerson, O.M., 'Use made of the revenue from the tax on tea', *New England Quarterly, 31*, 1958.

Gruber, I.D., 'Lord Howe and Lord George Germain: British Politics and the winning of American independence', *William and Mary Quarterly*, Third Series, *22*, 1965.

Hughes, E., ed., 'Lord North's Correspondence 1766–83', *English Historical Review, 62*, 1947.

Johnson, D.T., 'Charles James Fox: from government to opposition, 1771–1774', *English Historical Review, 89*, 1974.

Marshall, P., 'Lord Hillsborough, Samuel Wharton and the Ohio Grant, 1769–1775', *English Historical Review, 80*, 1965.

Roberts, M., 'Great Britain and the Swedish Revolution 1772–3', *Historical Journal, 7*, 1964.

Smith, C.D., 'Lord North's Posture of Defense', *Quarterly Journal of Speech, 45*, 1959.

Smith, C.D., 'Tracing the Correspondence of George III and Lord North', *Manuscripts, 14*, 1962.

Thomas, P.D.G., 'Sources for Debates of the House of Commons 1768–1774', *Bulletin Institute Historical Research, Special Supplement No. 4*, 1959.

Thomas, P.D.G., 'John Wilkes and the Freedom of the Press (1771)', *Bulletin Institute of Historical Research, 33*, 1960.

C. *Unpublished University Theses*

Brown, L.H., Lord North's relations with cabinet colleagues, 1767–1774. (B.Litt., Oxford, 1956.)

Hamer, M.T., From the Grafton Administration to the Ministry of North 1768–1772. (Ph.D., Cambridge, 1971.)

Tomlinson, J.R.G., The Grenville Papers 1763–1765. (M.A., Manchester, 1956.)

INDEX